Teaching Immigrant and Second-Language Students

STRATEGIES FOR SUCCESS

Edited by Michael Sadowski

HARVARD EDUCATION PRESS
CAMBRIDGE, MASSACHUSETTS

Second Printing, 2008

Library of Congress Control Number 2004108774

Paperback Edition: 978-1-891792-51-9
Library Edition: 978-1-891792-52-6

Published by Harvard Education Press,
an imprint of the Harvard Education Publishing Group

Harvard Education Press
8 Story Street
Cambridge, MA 02138

Typesetting: Sheila Walsh
Cover Design: Anne Carter
Cover Photo: Getty Images

The typefaces used in this book are Kuenstler 480 for text and Humanist 777 for display.

Contents

Introduction

Teaching the New Generation of U.S Students

Michael Sadowski

Ask any group of dedicated teachers, administrators, or school counselors to identify their most fundamental aspirations for their students and you're likely to tap into the sorts of passions that got them involved in education in the first place: "I want to help young people realize their full potential." "I want my students to become better thinkers and better people." "I want to prepare students for higher education so that they can have rewarding careers in whatever fields they choose."

The passions that drive our most committed educators in their work have not changed, but the landscape in which they are working to achieve these goals is changing rapidly. A recent analysis of U.S. Census data and other statistics by Donald J. Hernandez of the State University of New York at Albany (in press) points to the following trends:

- One in five children in the United States comes from an immigrant family (i.e., one or both of their parents were born outside the country).
- Children from immigrant families are the fastest-growing segment of the U.S. child population. Since 1990, their number has grown seven times faster than that of their counterparts from U.S.-born families.

- Immigration, once largely confined to a handful of states and urban centers, has been rising in virtually every U.S. state. Yet many states that have had low immigration rates historically have little institutional infrastructure to accommodate recent influxes of newcomer families.
- Whereas the vast majority of immigrants to the United States came from Europe and Canada at the beginning of the 20th century, today more than 80 percent of immigrant families come from Latin America and Asia.
- Children from immigrant families are more likely than their peers to live in poverty, to be behind in grade level, and to live in overcrowded housing.
- More than 70 percent of children from immigrant families speak a language other than English at home.

Given the linguistic and cultural diversity of today's school-age population—which will become even more diverse in the coming decades—it is becoming clearer every day that "education as usual" will not suffice. Simply put, good intentions—even when combined with vast subject-matter knowledge and a host of pedagogical strategies—are not enough. Educators can succeed in teaching the students of the new generation only if they understand linguistic and cultural diversity these students bring to the classroom and develop strategies that are informed by this understanding. With this in mind, the *Harvard Education Letter* has paid special attention in recent years to the trends in immigration, language, and culture that are changing U.S. education, and to the research and innovative practice that have begun to shed light on the most effective ways to educate this new generation of students.

In this volume, the second in the *Harvard Education Letter* Spotlight Series, we combine four articles that have appeared in the *Letter* since September/October 2002 with six new chapters written or adapted especially for this collection. The first part of the book's title, *Teaching Immigrant and Second-Language Students*, represents an admittedly imperfect attempt to capture the widely diverse population of students who are most affected by the recent demographic changes. As Hernandez and others remind us, not all immigrant students are English-language learners (ELLs), not all students from immigrant families are immigrants themselves (in fact, the majority are not), and many ELLs in U.S. schools were born in the United States. But issues associated with immigration, language acquisition, and cultural difference are central to the ways education has changed in recent years—and to the ways educators must rethink their practice to be able to serve *all* their students effectively in the years to come.

The second part of this volume's title, *Strategies for Success*, highlights the other main task our 13 authors take on— offering specific, practical ideas that teachers, administrators, and counselors (and, in a few cases, policymakers) can implement to bridge linguistic and cultural differences and create opportunities for today's diverse students to be successful in school and beyond.

In the book's opening chapter, Donald Freeman defines the task of "Teaching in the Context of English-Language Learners." Freeman notes that the currently prevailing system, whereby English as a Second Language (ESL) instruction is largely kept separate from "mainstream" classes, ignores the continuum of English-language learning that exists among today's students and separates ELLs from their English-fluent peers—and from the rigorous course content they need to achieve any real measure of academic success. Freeman argues that it is therefore the business of all educators, not just

ESL teachers, to understand what it means to teach in this new context so that ELLs can be full participants in the education that is available in their schools.

In Chapter 2, Evangeline Harris Stefanakis uses the example of kindergarten prescreening tests to illustrate how educators' lack of understanding about immigrant students' linguistic and cultural differences can result in misreading their abilities. She proposes a sociocultural approach to assessing students from immigrant families that draws on these children's backgrounds and strengths, rather than traditional assessment methods that often misdiagnose cultural and linguistic differences as deficits in skills and cognitive development.

Chapters 3 through 5 continue the discussion of teaching and assessment, highlighting strategies that can benefit students not just in their language development, but across the curriculum. In Chapter 3, Meg Gebhard, Andrew Habana Hafner, and Mary Wright profile Wright's innovative approach to mathematics instruction, which has helped her teach third-grade ELLs "The Language Game of Math." In Chapter 4, Mary T. Jeannot describes the linguistic and cultural challenges that immigrant and second-language students face as they confront standardized tests and—like Gebhard, Hafner, and Wright—presents strategies teachers can use to break down the barriers that often obscure students' true abilities. And in Chapter 5, Greta Vollmer discusses the ways teachers can use the linguistic and cultural transitions students from immigrant families experience as valuable material to help them deepen their writing skills.

Chapters 6 and 7 move to discussions of how teachers, administrators, and counselors can address the unique educational needs of two particular groups of students. Chapter 6 is devoted to the issues affecting immigrant students who have come to the United States as refugees. As author Shaun Sutner describes, post-traumatic stress disorder and other mental and emotional conditions can deeply affect the schooling experience of students whose families have fled war and violence in their countries of origin. In Chapter 7, Reino Makkonen describes the unique challenges students from migrant families face, including the educational discontinuity that results when their families move from place to place in search of work. As Makkonen also notes, a large percentage of migrant students come from immigrant families and experience linguistic and cultural barriers that compound the challenges of moving from school to school. Both Sutner and Makkonen profile schools that have implemented promising programs to help meet the specific needs of these student populations.

In addition to teachers, both principals and parents play important roles in the educational success of immigrant and second-language students. In Chapter 8, Maricel G. Santos highlights the leadership of several elementary school principals who have taken active steps to ensure that their schools support English-language learners effectively. In "Raising the Achievement of English-Language Learners: How Principals Can Make a Difference," Santos also offers a self-assessment that school leaders can use to evaluate their own leadership and schools. And in Chapter 9, "Bringing Parents on Board," Sue Miller Wiltz describes how schools can bridge linguistic and cultural differences to help immigrant parents be effective allies in their children's education.

Finally, in Chapter 10, "On Nobody's Agenda: Improving English-Language Learners' Access to Higher Education," Rebecca M. Callahan and Patricia Gándara consider the prospects for linguistically and culturally diverse students as they leave the preK–12 education system. Backed up by data that point to low rates of college attendance among immigrant students and English-language learners, Callahan and Gándara argue that too many educators have low expectations for these students and view high school graduation as an acceptable terminal goal. The authors end by proposing ways to transform schools so that they truly provide equal opportunity for students to thrive in college and in rewarding careers.

Many of the ideas put forth by these authors call upon teachers, administrators, and counselors to rethink fundamental aspects of their work. The authors do not suggest, however, that educators need to do more just to achieve the same results they have been achieving all along. Rather, they make a strong collective case that the linguistic and cultural diversity of today's preK–12 student population offers U.S. educators not just a challenge, but an opportunity to expand the definition of what it means to teach students effectively. They underscore the need for all young people in today's increasingly global society to develop a wider understanding of language, culture, and community. They also highlight the vast potential of language and culture to build bridges to new kinds of learning, understanding, and achievement—not just for English-language learners or children from immigrant families, but for all students in our schools.

REFERENCE

Hernandez, D. J. (in press). Demographic change and the life circumstances of immigrant families. *Future of Children*.

CHAPTER 1

Teaching in the Context of English-Language Learners

What Do We Need to Know?

Donald Freeman

AN OLD REALITY, A NEW NORM

Classrooms in the United States are changing. Though the pressures may seem more dramatic and widespread now than in the past, teachers are in fact responding to changes similar to those they have faced since the advent of institutionalized, publicly funded schooling in the early 1800s (Tyack & Cuban, 1995). U.S. public schools have always enrolled immigrant students. In various periods, these newly arrived students have been the focal point of public education. At the turn of the 20th century, for example, urban communities, primarily in the Northeast and northern Midwest, saw the arrival of large numbers of immigrants. A century ago, their numbers ranged from 450,000 in 1900 to 1.25 million in 1907, most of them from Eastern Europe and the Mediterranean (U.S. Census Bureau, 1975). Schools were at the center of that socialization, as Nancy Hoffman notes in *Woman's "True" Profession* (2003), a collection of accounts of teachers' lives in the last two centuries:

> Like her sister teachers of nineteenth-century rural New England, the teacher of immigrants was expected to shape character, impart the rudiments of good citizenship, and prepare her charges for vocations. . . . Of the newly arrived immigrants, most did not speak English; many could not read or write in their home languages, and any number came from cultures of which the teacher herself was ignorant. Without special approaches to teaching non-English speakers a second language, the teacher forged ahead in English with a curriculum modified only slightly from the work of the New England schoolmen. Her students' first English words were her words; their first American ideas, her interpretation of American morals, manners, and culture. (p. 229)

Hoffman's historical documentary research speaks to the power and influence of education generally and of the teacher specifically in socializing newly arrived students and in introducing them to English as the language of instruction. Even while this historical image of schools as socially and linguistically homogenizing institutions is again becoming politically popular, we face the question of how schools and teachers can best support students who come from different cultural and educational backgrounds, and who do not share English as the medium of social participation and instruction.

The following statistics on English-language learners in the United States put this situation in more recent perspective:

- Students from non-English-speaking backgrounds represent the fastest-growing segment of the school-age population. The U.S. Office of English Language Achievement survey reported that, in the decade from 1990 to 2001, the number of English-language learners enrolled in U.S. public schools grew 105 percent (Kindler, 2002).
- The U.S. Census Bureau (2000) reports that roughly one in five school-age children are English-language learners.

Beneath the surface of these national numbers lies a more complicated story, one that challenges some popular misperceptions. First, one might think, as did students in the early 1900s, that the majority of English-language learners today come from immigrant homes. They do not. This misperception that immigration equates with multilingualism in schools, as some political arguments contend, does not bear up. For example, the number of second-generation Latino students entering U.S. schools will more than double by 2020, so that the majority of these students who will need English-language support will be born in the United States (Suro & Passel, 2003).

Second, one might think that the challenge of educating English-language learners is an urban phenomenon, or that it is geographically confined to particular regions of the United States. Again, that is not the case. In Vermont, for example, a state with limited cultural, racial, and linguistic diversity, 50 languages other than English are spoken by roughly 1,100 children across the state. These numbers, combined with the state's rural character, produce a fuller picture of the complex demands of this situation. Although the total number of English-language learners is quite small (these 1,100 children make up about one percent of the state's total school-age population), the impact is far reaching: More than two-thirds of Vermont's school districts (47 of 62) enroll students whose home language is not English (National Clearinghouse for English Language Acquisition, 2001). Although they may be only a few students per grade or school, the legal and educational demands to meet their learning needs are no less pressing.

So the challenge to communities and elected officials, to schools and administrators, and to teachers in classrooms is clear: Serving students who are English-language learners is widespread and becoming more so, and serving these students means knowing how to teach them.

WHAT DOES IT MEAN TO TEACH IN THE CONTEXT OF ENGLISH-LANGUAGE LEARNERS?

An April 2004 editorial in the *Los Angeles Times* traces the trajectory of this educational challenge very clearly:

> The acronyms help tell the story. Years ago, they were ESL children, immigrant children for whom English was a second language. Then they were renamed LEP, for their limited English proficiency. Today those same kids are dubbed ELL, or English-language learners. The labels have changed to reflect educational fashion, and classroom methods have followed suit—from the simple language and broad gestures used by English-speaking teachers in ESL classes, to bilingual programs taught by bicultural instructors, to the English-only classes instituted across California by electoral fiat. But the fundamental problems that keep immigrant kids from catching up seem stubbornly resistant to change. ("Long Road to Fluency," p. 20).

The editorial goes on to comment on the difference in academic progress between students fluent in English and English-language learners in recent California high-stakes assessments and then cogently observes: "But there is a difference between learning English and learning *in* English. . . . Too many kids are stacking up just short of [English] fluency, lacking the skills necessary to understand photosynthesis, appreciate Shakespeare, or calculate a word problem in an algebra class" (p. 20).

The distinction between learning English and learning *in* English goes to the heart of the educational challenge. A good deal is known about how English-language learners "learn" in general classrooms. "Learn" here refers to how they participate, how they can participate more successfully, and—indeed in the context of the federal No Child Left Behind legislation—how they fare on various standardized assessments. This knowledge base has been derived from research in several domains— studies of instructed second-language acquisition, of classroom discourse, of literacy instruction, of classroom participation patterns and structures, and from studies of the teaching of various subjects (mathematics and science, for instance). While the findings are rich (as is demonstrated in other chapters in this collection), the principal weakness is that the research has not been assembled as comprehensively and coherently as it could—and should—be. So the issue is not *whether* there is a knowledge base for how to teach English-language learners; there is one. The issue is *how* that knowledge base is learned, distributed among, and used by all teachers.

This is what is meant by the title of this chapter, "Teaching in the Context of English-Language Learners." Traditionally, educational models and practices have defined the teaching of English-language learners as a specialized undertaking, as the province of the ESL and/or bilingual teacher. This view has been buttressed by the specialized training, knowledge, and skills that these ESL and/or bilingual teachers bring to their work, as well as by the organization of schools that usually separates English-language learners from their English-fluent peers and supports ESL instruction as a distinct form of teaching, both in time (as in pull-out or ESL-only classes) and in space (as in separate ESL classrooms). Social evidence suggests, however, that this specialized knowledge/instruction approach has largely run its course in the United States, due to a convergence of factors. These include state mandates and local policies that are dismantling bilingual education and straight ESL instruction, as well as federal policies that mandate assessment of all students, including English-language learners. All of this is occurring in the context of shrinking financial resources that are limiting funds available for specialized ESL instruction. And driving the shift most fundamentally are the simple forces of demographics summarized earlier: that more and more students need English-language support in order to have access to what is taught and to be educationally successful.

In addition, the demographics of the United States make it abundantly clear that most teachers do—or shortly will—teach classes that combine students who are English-language learners at various stages of fluency with other students who are fluent in English. Thus, what has been seen as a *difference in kind* between English-language learners and their English-fluent peers is now increasingly experienced in most schools as a *difference of degree*. Many classrooms have students who range on a scale from limited English proficient to English fluent. Where individual students fall on this scale, and how they progress along it, changes over time, and classroom instruction needs to meet this variety in English-language proficiency. The implications for teaching and learning are clear: Teaching English-language learners is less and less a specialized responsibility; their instruction is now increasingly shared by all teachers.

This is an instructional challenge that most teachers feel ill prepared and insufficiently supported to meet. A 1999–2000 survey of schools and staffing by the National Center for Education Statistics (2001) found that, while 41 percent of the three million teachers surveyed reported teaching English-language learners, only 12.5 percent had received more than eight hours (or the equivalent of one work day) of training in how to do so. The shift that is required, then, is to transform the teaching of English-language learners from a specialized activity to one that is shared—or distributed—among most (if not all) teachers in a given school. The argument for such a shift can be summed up as follows:

- Teaching English-language learners has largely been a discrete undertaking, the domain of ESL and bilingual teachers, conceived as a differentiated set of practices based on a specialized knowledge base of classroom instruction.
- That design is changing for many reasons. In some senses, we have in the United States a gathering "perfect storm" of policy and legal changes, diminishing financial and human resources, and new student demographics that are propelling the change.

- The job of teaching English-language learners is thus becoming less the province of specialization; it must be more and more generally distributed throughout the school.

INCLUSION AND IMMERSION: TWO METAPHORS FRAMING THE CURRENT DEBATE

This redistribution of responsibility means that the linguistic dimension of the classroom becomes more critical in instruction. In the current debate, there are two ways in which the linguistic dimensions of teaching are often talked about in policy, research, and classroom practice. Each term proposes, or carries in it, a metaphor for how the key elements of learner and instruction fit together. And, as is true with any words, the terms also echo other historical versions of that connection.

Inclusion is one of these terms. It focuses on the learners themselves. To say that English-language learners are "included" in mainstream classes or teaching speaks to how these students participate in the normative, English-medium classroom. The term draws on the history of separation or exclusion through a lack of appropriate support that English-language learners have faced because of their lack of English fluency. As a concept, inclusion references, to some extent, the perspectives of special education and the legal precedents of the Individuals with Disabilities in Education Act (IDEA) and its predecessor, Public Law 99, which hold that learning-disabled students should be educated in the "least restrictive environment." Echoes of this "inclusive/exclusive" thinking can be found, for example, where English-language learners are categorized as needing special education because of their lack of English fluency. Such situations, while not uncommon,[1] are complicated by the difficulties of accurately assessing a student's learning needs in multiple languages. (For a discussion of the way screenings often inaccurately identify English-language learners as students with special needs, see Chapter 2.)

The second term—*immersion*—in contrast foregrounds curriculum and instruction over learners. To say that English-language learners are "immersed" in mainstream classrooms describes their experience from the perspective of the content and instruction that they are receiving. Immersion speaks of students who are placed—either completely or on a limited basis—in a completely English-medium instructional environment, which is new to them, and they are expected to learn the content in that classroom environment just as their English-fluent peers do. The term draws on references to language immersion, in which students enter into a new language primarily through content.[2] This term, and its various attendant instructional practices and curricular designs, has become a popular remedy of choice in the political world for many reasons. Some parents see immersion as the accelerated route to a full education in English for their children; some politicians and policymakers see it as a "cost-effective" way to incorporate English-language learners from a wide variety of language backgrounds into general instruction.

Placed side-by-side, these terms frame two perspectives on how English-language learners enter into classrooms in English. *Inclusion* focuses on the dynamics of their classroom and social participation; it suggests metaphorically that those who have been left out are brought in. *Immersion*, on the other hand, focuses on how the content of lessons and curricula are organized and the language in which this content is taught. Immersion carries a metaphorical sense of water, of the challenge that the content and medium present to the learner to "sink or swim." Interestingly, the newly prevalent term, especially in Massachusetts, is *sheltered immersion* (Massachusetts Department of Education, 2004). This is a sort of hybrid phrase that combines the notion of sheltering (with its roots in the disability literature) with that of immersion (which has a linguistic heritage). So in a way, sheltered immersion speaks both to how English-language learners participate in lessons and to the curricular content and medium in which they are taking part.

All three terms—inclusion, immersion, and sheltered immersion—focus a newfound attention on the linguistic dimension of teaching and learning, regardless of who the learner is. This shift in thinking to address the linguistic dimension of academic content is no small feat; in fact, it seems to be a sea change. Consider the three general constituencies of teachers who must do so—ESL teachers, bilingual teachers, and general classroom teachers. Each group is trained to adopt a particular view of the role of language in instruction. ESL teachers focus primarily on their students' acquisition of English-language skills (at times to the reduction of classroom content) with the thinking that, once a sufficient foundation in English has been established, access to academic content can follow. Bilingual teachers focus on the home or community languages as a vehicle to academic content, in the thinking that content can be learned in and potentially transferred from one language to another. And classroom teachers focus on integrating social participation and grade-level or subject-specific content, often with little attention to the linguistic medium in which they are teaching. Thus each group has a piece of the language/content puzzle, but no one sees or addresses the whole picture.

Understanding the role of language in academic content has become a central feature in teaching; it has to inform curriculum and lesson planning, and it has to shape instruction. If teaching in the context of English-language learners is a fully distributed responsibility in education, then it will require a shift in how teachers conceive of academic content, how they teach it, and how they assess it. In the context of U.S. standards-based reform efforts, this change is a significant one. Whether one agrees with the legislation or not, the federal No Child Left Behind law has had the effect of making visible the academic progress of English-language learners. So as states articulate content standards and instruments to assess those standards, they are also having to grapple with defining the English language necessary for students to have access to those standards (Abedi, 2004).

A CHANGE IN VIEW

Whether inclusion or immersion, there is a fundamental change embedded in this view that teaching English-language learners is a responsibility shared by all teachers. The change moves from viewing students' lack of English-language skills as a deficit to be remediated—after which English-language learners can "function like other kids"—to viewing students' fluency in English as ranging along a natural continuum from instructionally fluent in English to needing support. And such support is not necessarily confined to the classic ESL services. It also ranges from support for literacy among young learners in preschool and elementary school, whose entry in reading may vary regardless of their home language (Heath, 1983); to support for all students in middle school as they move from direct instruction in reading and writing to more genre-based assignments in science, English, and social studies; to writing across the curriculum for high school students to improve the quality of written language (Calkins, 1986).

When we view the linguistic variations between English-language learners and their English-fluent classmates as a difference *in kind*, we reinforce this deficit view. This gives rise to and supports a differentiated—or segregated—educational model in which ESL teachers teach English-language learners, and once these students become fluent in English (and their "deficit" has been addressed), "mainstream" or general education teachers take over. This view is no longer tenable from the standpoint of human and financial resources, let alone the quality of educational practice and student learning.

Language is an instructional medium, a conveyor or medium of content, a structurer of classroom activity and participation, a network of social interaction both among students and between students and teacher, a mediator of identities—the list is rich and varied. There is much work—in research and policy, in how schools are run, in how teachers are supported—that needs to be redone, rethought, and understood in new ways. Students who are English-language learners present us with the classic challenge/opportunity to rethink what we are doing and to do it better.

For these reasons, we need to redefine the educational challenge. We must understand "teaching in the context of English-language learners" as a general educational practice and a distributed professional responsibility. English-language learners represent an increasing student presence that all teachers need to learn to understand and to teach effectively. As a community, we need to better understand what this distribution of educational responsibility demands of teachers, what it means to learners, and how it shapes our classrooms, schools, and communities. This will call for new definitions of educators' work and new forms of support throughout the educational system.

REFERENCES

Abedi, J. (2004). The "No Child Left Behind Act" and English language learners: Assessment and accountability issues. *Educational Researcher, 33*, 4–14.

Becker, H. (2001). *Teaching ESL k–12: Views from the classroom*. Boston: Heinle and Heinle.

Calkins, L. M. (1986). *The art of teaching writing*. Portsmouth, NH: Heinemann.

Heath, S. B. (1983). *Ways of words: Language and work in communities and classrooms*. New York: Cambridge University Press.

Hoffman, N. (2003). *Woman's "true" profession: Voices from the history of teaching* (2nd ed.). Cambridge, MA: Harvard Education Press.

Kindler, A. L. (2002). *Survey of the states' limited English proficient students and available educational programs and services, 2000–2001 summary report*. Washington, DC: Office of English Language Acquisition and Language Instruction Educational Programs.

The long road to fluency [Editorial]. (2004, April 3). *Los Angeles Times*, p. 20B.

Massachusetts Department of Education. (2004). *English language proficiency benchmarks and outcomes*. Malden, MA: Author.

National Center for Education Statistics. (2001). *Schools and staffing survey, 1999–2000*. Washington, DC: Author.

National Clearinghouse for English Language Acquisition. (2001). *Vermont data and demographics*. Available online at http://www.ncela.gwu.edu/policy/states/vermont/index.htm.

Suro, R., & Pasel, J. (2003). *The rise of the second generation: Changing patterns in Hispanic population growth*. Washington, DC: Pew Hispanic Center.

Swain, M. (1985). Communicative competence: Some rules for comprehensible input and comprehensible output in development. In S. Gass & C. Madden (Eds.), *Input in second language acquisition* (pp. 235–253). Rowley, MA: Newbury House.

Tyack, D., & Cuban, L. (1995). *Tinkering toward Utopia: A century of public school reform*. Cambridge, MA: Harvard University Press.

U.S. Census Bureau. (1975). *Historical statistics of the United States, colonial times to 1970*. Washington, DC: Author.

U.S. Census Bureau. (2000). *Table 2: Language use, English ability, and linguistic isolation for the population 5 to 17 years by state: 2000*. Retrieved May 1, 2004, from http://www.census.gov/population/cen2000/phc-t20/tab02.pdf.

NOTES

1. For discussion of this issue, see Becker (2001, ch. 6).
2. For example, see the classic discussion in Swain (1985).

CHAPTER 2

Assessing Young Immigrant Students

Are We Finding Their Strengths?

Evangeline Harris Stefanakis

ean-Yves' story is set in 2002, the year the Commonwealth of Massachusetts hired me for the second time as a consultant to the Boston and Somerville public schools.* I was commissioned to address the difficulties associated with screening limited-English-speaking children for special needs identification and to devise "creative" ways of testing these students. Having been a special educator in the United States and abroad, I understood the limitations of formal testing and knew that language strongly affected a child's performance on such screenings.

I thought I had a simple agenda as I set off to observe kindergarten screenings in a Boston public school. Children and mothers were arriving for the scheduled preschool test of three- to five-year-olds. On the advice of a school specialist, I followed Jean-Yves, a four-year-old Haitian child, and his

---

*Jean-Yves is a pseudonym.

translator through the screening process. Although I know French, not Creole, I could both see and understand that this child did not want to leave his mother, despite the adults urging him to come along.

The translator, a young male teacher, took the reluctant child by the hand while the mother said a short farewell and urged him to "listen to the teacher." (My French helped me to decipher this statement.) Jean-Yves held the translator's hand and listened to assurances, in Creole, that they were "just going to play games." He walked with his head and eyes down and was met by a female speech-and-language therapist. She ushered the child and the translator into a tiny room labeled Station #1, and they took their places in the room's two empty chairs. The therapist spoke in English to the translator, who said the child seemed to understand Creole.

The therapist began administering the language portion of the test to Jean-Yves, including questions about his name and about various body parts. The translator patiently repeated the questions in Creole, but Jean-Yves simply looked down and remained silent. The translator told the therapist that these questions were hard for the child. He suggested that Jean-Yves be asked to tell a story about his mother and family. The child remained quiet with eyes wide, but said nothing. The therapist gave the translator paper for Jean-Yves to draw his family. He still did not respond to the translator's suggestions, given in Creole, to draw or to talk. The score sheet was marked "untestable," and the boy and his translator went on to the next station.

At Station #2, the special education teacher sat in a large classroom with puzzles and blocks on the table. Again, Jean-Yves and the translator sat across from the specialist. The

. specialist and translator chatted for a minute, then a few toys were brought out to entice the child to play. No response. Both the translator and the tester decided to try some segments of the test.

The tester asked Jean-Yves for a red block, then a blue block. When the child did not respond, the translator offered him some blocks to hold. Jean-Yves handled a block or two, then started to make a tower. He did not follow through on the commands of the tester or the translator, who then tried to show him pictures and puzzles. The child looked away, shook his leg, and waited. Once again, the score sheet was marked "untestable," and the boy and his translator were ushered to the next station. The child traveled the circuit, "failed" the hearing test, and was deemed "untestable" on all other portions of the testing that day.

"UNTESTABLE" OR CULTURALLY DIFFERENT?

I watched as the translator finished with Jean-Yves, then we went out to the play area where other mothers were waiting. I asked the translator if this child's performance was typical of what he saw when he worked in Boston. He confirmed that it was and said he believed many Haitian children were frightened and were not used to doing what adults asked of them in school. He told me that many of the parents he meets often tell their children to "behave," and that means to "be quiet." So he felt that many of these children needed more time than they were usually given to get used to the teachers and to feel comfortable talking.

My next observation puzzled me further. I turned and saw Jean-Yves, who had just been labeled "untestable," playing in the waiting area. He was very animated with the other children. I heard them laughing. I saw the children handling toys and interacting with each other verbally while the mothers chatted and the school staff milled around. Who would see Jean-Yves speaking and happily interacting with other children while he played?

Jean-Yves' mother was given a slip of paper that said he needed to be retested in three months to determine if he had special needs. But the question remained in my mind, especially given the ease with which Jean-Yves interacted with the other children: Was he tested correctly *this* time? Or did some form of cultural misunderstanding impede the process?

ARE WE FINDING ASSETS OR DEFICITS?

Jean-Yves' story is not an isolated incident. Currently, one in five public school students in the United States is either the child of immigrant parents or is an immigrant her- or himself. Yet it is far too easy for these children, especially those whose dominant language is not English, to "fail" preschool screening and later testing and to enter school with the label "special needs."

Researchers have known for years that English-language learners are regularly misidentified for special education placement. "Once a referral is made, the likelihood of testing is high. Once testing takes place, strong gravitational forces toward special education placement are in motion," wrote Genevieve Fedoruk (1989), author of numerous studies in the 1980s and 1990s. "Once a language-minority child is referred for testing, that same child is placed in special education about 85 percent of the time. Once a child is placed in special education, despite a mistaken assessment, it takes them on average six years to get out."

In addition, researchers have long agreed that standardized testing done in the context of a "child deficit model"—looking for deficiencies in a child's abilities—may do more harm than good, especially for language-minority students. "Children may be temporarily overwhelmed by difficulties or blocked in their expression, but that does not mean that they cannot be helped to develop their strengths," noted Anne Martin in a 1988 *Harvard Educational Review* article. "Predicting failure can be a way to ensure it."

Still, federal law mandates that language-minority children be screened for special needs before they enter school, and the screening formats used are often culturally biased, dated, or both. In Boston, for example, the Early Screening Test Instrument (ESI) is used to screen all children, despite serious limitations. The ESI, originally developed using a population of 700 white, middle-class children from Rhode Island, had no minorities in its sample. And, according to the manual, the reliability and validity testing of the measurement were done in 1972.

So how can language-minority students be assessed in ways that help them to "develop their strengths" rather than label them as deficient? The first step involves looking carefully at the interaction between teacher and learner. This suggests redefining the purposes, formats, and processes associated with the assessment of diverse language learners.

COMPLEX DIFFERENCES, COMPLEX SOLUTIONS

The traditional psychometric model of formal assessment used to evaluate all children consists of standardized tests and other fixed techniques to diagnose language and learning problems. These tools assume that any deficit that might be detected is in the child. This model contrasts with a sociocultural approach, which assumes that every child presents a unique example of difference and complexity, and that understanding the difference—not the deficit—is the role of educational assessment.

A sociocultural perspective assumes that children learn language in real-life situations that depend on social interactions, and that bilingual children display different knowledge and language uses depending on the social contexts in which they are learning and living. In addition, a sociocultural perspective rests on three premises:

1. Bilingualism is a cognitive asset that enhances thinking and learning.
2. Sociocultural factors affect learning, and the context, or learning environment, is key to understanding language use.
3. Language proficiency and individual learning abilities should be assessed in context and over time.

Within this framework, classroom assessment becomes an interactive process where teachers "sit beside" children to assess and teach them. This approach to assessment realigns the usual power relationship between the potentially dominant teacher and the dominated child. Both what teachers do and what students do during learning activities are examined, simultaneously and not in isolation. Thus, assessment becomes a four-step process whereby the teacher:

1. self-assesses and researches the child's language and culture;
2. assesses the language demands of the classroom;
3. probes for the child's individual learning strengths;

**ASSESSING LANGUAGE-MINORITY STUDENTS:
A SOCIOCULTURAL APPROACH**

1. Assess your own knowledge, then research the child's language and culture.
2. Assess the language demands of the classroom.
3. Probe for the child's individual learning strengths.
4. Gather data on the child by monitoring his or her daily interactions in various groups within the classroom.

4. gathers data on the child by monitoring his or her daily interactions in various groups within the classroom.

A sociocultural approach to assessment examines both the process and the products of a language-minority student's learning. Teachers examine the complexity of a child's background social and cultural factors (who a child is and how they learn); political factors (how a child reacts in a particular environment or setting); linguistic factors (how a child uses both native and second languages); and academic/educational factors (how a child performs a given task).

Overall, this framework suggests that educators look not only at what is "wrong" with the child, but also at what is "wrong" about what *they* know about language and culture, as well as the learning environment itself (the school, the classroom, or the curriculum).

PORTFOLIO ASSESSMENT: PROCESS AND PRODUCT

To address the need for a more comprehensive and complete assessment of language-minority children, educators in many urban schools have begun using a portfolio assessment approach. The concept is to combine formal and informal assessment materials with a variety of observational sources to create a more complete picture of the strengths and weaknesses of young children as learners.

For language-minority children, the process involves collecting a "portfolio of information" that draws on a variety of sources, from observations of classroom work and play to questionnaires completed by parents. By compiling a wide range of data about a child, educators can gain a more comprehensive understanding of the child and her or his skills.

Before a child is involved in the screening or testing process, a parent interview helps determine the child's preferred language. For limited-English-proficient children, a speech-and-language specialist performs language-dominance testing. All observations, tests, and interviews are then administered in the child's dominant language. In the Somerville and Boston programs, testing personnel are available to test students in English and Spanish. For children who speak languages other than Spanish, translators who speak the child's language accompany the testers.

Teams that include administrators, facilitators, special educators, speech-and-language pathologists, occupational therapists, parent liaisons, and kindergarten teachers work in groups to develop each system's customized portfolio approach to screening and assessment. The basic framework for each school system's portfolio assessment includes:

- observation of play behavior by two or three teachers and/or other school personnel
- observation of group interaction using a formal checklist
- a preschool screening or testing instrument

- a parent questionnaire and follow-up interview
- research on the child's culture of origin

In school systems where this approach has been used, administrators, teachers, and specialists agree that children's assets or strengths are identified more often than in single-screening test efforts. The portfolio process also provides multiple perspectives on each child, thereby validating learning areas that may show culturally biased differences.

MULTIPLE LANGUAGES, MULTIPLE ASSESSMENTS

The use of a portfolio approach to preschool screening may offer a means of assessment that can more carefully discern language from learning problems. If language-minority children are not mislabeled as special education students early on, they stand a better chance of thriving in a mainstream academic environment later on.

Screening and standardized testing practices in the United States are often discriminatory, and the testing of language-minority students represents a special case of bias. Limited-English-proficient children who are screened and later tested using standardized measures are too often labeled deficient. Respecting language and cultural differences, as well as variability in child development, requires looking carefully at the strengths of immigrant children. Respecting the variability of child development and the realities of language and cultural differences means looking carefully at immigrant children for their strengths. Sometimes early differences in child development may appear similar to characteristics of some disabilities, but a more careful look can often lead to different conclusions.

Language-acquisition issues are key variables that need to be ruled out before educators determine whether a child has a disability. But can realistic assessments be performed with children like Jean-Yves on the first day they enter a school building? We need to allow children time in school—time to develop language, and time to understand the expectations of their teachers and their schools.

We also need to consider alternative approaches to teaching, learning, and assessment so that we can find the best in *all* children who attend our schools. At a minimum, a sociocultural framework for teaching and learning and a portfolio approach to assessment can help educators gather a variety of information about language-minority children and how they learn. Approaches like these are the only ways we will truly be able to teach and reach all children.

This chapter was supported by a grant from the Foundation for Child Development. It originally appeared in the May/June 2004 issue of the Harvard Education Letter.

REFERENCES

Fedoruk, G. M. (1989). Kindergarten screening for 1st-grade learning problems: The conceptual inadequacy of a child-deficit model. *Childhood Education, 66,* 40–42.

Martin, A. (1988). Screening, early intervention, and remediation: Obscuring children's potential. *Harvard Educational Review, 58,* 488–501.

FOR FURTHER INFORMATION

D. August and K. Hakuta. *Improving Schooling for Language Minority Children: A Research Agenda.* Washington, DC: National Academy Press, 1997.

L.M. Baca and H.T. Cervantes. *The Bilingual Special Education Interface* (3rd ed.). Upper Saddle River, NJ: Merrill, 1998.

Center for Research on Education, Diversity & Excellence, University of California, Santa Cruz, 1156 High Street, Santa Cruz, CA 95064; tel. 831-459-3500. www.crede.org

The Education Alliance at Brown University, 222 Richmond Street, Suite 300, Providence, RI 02903; tel. 401-274-9548. www.alliance.brown.edu

J.M. O'Malley and L. Valdez Pierce. *Authentic Assessment for English-Language Learners: Practical Approaches for Teachers*. Reading, MA: Addison-Wesley, 1996.

B. Perez and M.E. Torres-Guzman. *Learning in Two Worlds: An Integrated Spanish/English Biliteracy Approach* (3rd ed.). Boston: Allyn & Bacon, 2002.

M. Suárez-Orozco and C. Suárez-Orozco. *Children of Immigration*. Cambridge, MA: Harvard University Press, 2001.

CHAPTER 3

Teaching English-Language Learners "The Language Game of Math"

Insights for Teachers and Teacher Educators

*Meg Gebhard, Andrew Habana Hafner,
and Mary Wright*

I n September 2003, nine-year-old Marisol Rivera hesitant-
ly entered Mary Wright's third-grade classroom at Sullivan
Elementary School in Holyoke, Massachusetts. Mary recalled her first impression of Marisol as a quiet, thought-
ful girl who seemed tentative and unsure of herself, particularly when it came to math. Mary quickly noticed that during
math, Marisol often hid behind other students and avoided
eye contact, which made it hard to determine how much she
understood. After checking school records and talking with
Marisol's former teachers about her schooling experiences,
Mary figured there probably were a number of reasons why
Marisol was trying to make herself "invisible."

Since moving to Holyoke from Puerto Rico three years earlier, Marisol had attended content classes where she received

some support in her native Spanish, while also getting assistance in learning English as a second language. However, Mary recalled that Marisol's teachers grew concerned with the rate of her progress and decided that she should repeat second grade and receive assistance from the special education team for what they described as "processing problems in language arts and math."

With this background information, Mary reflected on Marisol's participation in her class during the first several months of school, but she still wasn't sure what the problem was: Was it English? Was it math? Was it something else? It was hard to say, but what Mary was certain about was the need to rethink the way she was teaching the English-language learners (ELLs) in her class, especially the way she was teaching math.

This need became even more evident in 2002 with two major shifts in education policy at the federal and state levels. In January, President Bush signed the federal No Child Left Behind Act, and the following November voters passed anti-bilingual education legislation in Massachusetts. With these changes, Mary and her students were being held accountable—sometimes publicly in local and major newspapers—for meeting new state and federal standards in a language that many children were still in the process of acquiring.

The challenges students and teachers like Marisol and Mary face in their day-to-day work are not uncommon. They are the same problems facing a growing number of linguistically and culturally diverse students and their teachers, particularly in communities across the United States with histories similar to Holyoke's. Holyoke is a midsize former industrial city that during most of the 1900s supported a predominantly white immigrant community by providing readily available work in the city's paper mills. Over the last 30 years, nearly all of these mills have closed, but new businesses have not taken their place. Many of the skilled, better-paying jobs have also moved elsewhere, resulting in an unemployment rate that has doubled in the last three years from 4.2 percent to 8.4 percent. These trends have placed incredible stress on families and the available social service agencies in the community. Moreover, the families that rely on Holyoke's public schools to put their children on a path toward better-paying work are more linguistically, racially, and culturally diverse than three decades ago. The overall population of Holyoke in 2003 was described as 54 percent "non-Hispanic white," 41 percent "Latino" (mostly Puerto Rican), 4 percent "African American," and one percent "Asian." The school population, however, is 72 percent Latino.

The degree to which educators in many communities are ill equipped to address the complex challenges of supporting linguistically and culturally diverse students is illustrated in the 2003 math scores on the Massachusetts Comprehensive Assessment System (MCAS), the state's standardized testing program. These data show that 68 percent of all fourth graders scored in the "needs improvement" or "failing" category, and that failure rates are even higher at the upper grade levels. In 2003, almost no eighth-grade students in Holyoke (ELL or otherwise) scored "proficient" in math (37% scored in the "needs improvement" category, and 63% were considered "failing"). Clearly, this level of systemic failure is an enormous problem for educators, administrators, researchers, and policymakers who take the goal of social and economic equity through education seriously. It is also the problem that brought the authors of this chapter together.

THE ACCELA ALLIANCE

Meg Gebhard is an assistant professor at the University of Massachusetts and codirector of a school-based teacher education program called the ACCELA Alliance (Access to Critical Content and English Language Acquisition). The ACCELA Alliance is a federally funded partnership among the University of Massachusetts Amherst, three area school districts, and the diverse communities in Western Massachusetts. During the 2003–2004 academic year, Meg taught a two-semester course in second-language acquisition and academic literacy development. First, she assigned case studies written by leading education researchers who have studied the academic literacy development of linguistically and culturally diverse students in urban schools. She assigned these readings to give teachers an introduction to important debates in the teaching of reading and writing to English-language learners. Second, and more importantly, these readings provided teachers with detailed descriptions of classroom practices that either supported and/or constrained ELLs in learning to read and write in academic ways (e.g., drawing on prior knowledge and home-language abilities; providing an array of authentic purposes and real audiences for writing; providing models of good writing and analyzing its elements; creating opportunities for students to collaborate and receive feedback from peers and teachers). Meg hoped teachers would use these readings as models to develop their own research questions related to understanding more fully how their ELLs learned to read and write across the curriculum.

Mary Wright was a recipient of an ACCELA master's degree scholarship and a student in Meg's course. She grew up in Holyoke and had been working there for most of her 15-

year career as a classroom teacher. During the 2003–2004 school year, Mary taught a third-grade class with 25 students, two-thirds of whom were Latino and almost half of whom were in the process of learning English as a second language. Mary described teaching this class as one of the greatest challenges of her career because of her students' range of experiences and abilities. She had ELLs whose prior schooling experiences in Puerto Rico had equipped them to speed through skill-based worksheets quickly and accurately, but who had difficulty with the district's required math curriculum. This curriculum centered on teaching mathematical problem-solving rather than computational speed and accuracy. She had other students who were fluent English speakers. These students had experience with more process-oriented approaches to learning math, but really didn't have either the skill or conceptual base they needed to approach some of the tasks Mary was required to assign.

Mary describes the math hour as the time of the day when "it all came out." She says, "If someone is having a bad day, it'll show up in math. I know I'm going to get more bathroom requests, more fights, and more tears than any other time of the day." This level of anxiety was not limited to students, but extended to teachers and administrators because of an ongoing investigation by the state. (The state Department of Education was considering taking over the district in the wake of low test scores.)

Collectively, these classroom-, district-, and state-level pressures led Mary to focus her research questions on how to teach the language and content of this new math curriculum in the climate of high-stakes testing. In a journal assignment for Meg's class, Mary wrote:

I have begun to take advantage of students' normal curiosity about the MCAS test. . . . They know they have to take this test every year until 10th grade, and that their ability to graduate from high school depends on this test. . . . I keep telling them they are all very capable and they will pass the test . . . [but] I have to start teaching them about the types of open-ended word problems they are going to get—how to spot them and how to respond to them. We have started calling this a game, the language game of math. Third graders love games and can relate to the idea that if you know the rules, you can win.

To support Mary in exploring this central focus, Andrew Habana Hafner, a former classroom teacher and first-year doctoral student at the University of Massachusetts Amherst, visited Mary's class twice a month between September 2003 and May 2004. During these visits, he recorded digital video of students participating in math activities, collected samples of student work, provided transcripts of selected classroom interactions, and wrote detailed notes regarding how students' school days took shape. He also conducted informal interviews with students in Spanish and English.

Meg guided Drew and Mary as they collected data to inventory and analyze the kinds of reading and writing activities Marisol and other students had to accomplish in math. Next, she asked them to describe vocabulary, grammatical constructions, phrases, and organizational schemes that were particular to the third-grade math curriculum. In conducting an analysis of the language of math, Mary identified a task that she regularly assigned to students called "show your thinking." This was a multistep task that asked students to (a) read a mathematical word problem; (b) draw a picture representing the elements of the problem; (c) describe in narrative form how they would solve the problem; (d) write a corresponding mathematical formula; and (e) solve the equation correctly. The skills associated with this task were especially important for students to develop because Mary learned that almost all of the ELLs in her school had either skipped this open-ended section of the fourth-grade math MCAS or thought it was a multiple-choice question and responded accordingly.

USING LANGUAGE ARTS METHODS TO TEACH MATH

After reflecting on students' literacy inventories and aspects of her classroom practices, Mary realized that her students' math performance depended not just on their developing the kinds of skills traditionally associated with arithmetic, but on their language development as well. She began to apply language arts methods to teaching a content area that she previously associated only with numbers and symbols. Beginning in the fall of 2003, Mary instituted the following changes in her math program:

Grouping students by language and math ability. Mary grouped students heterogeneously by language and math ability so that they could share expertise and support each other in learning both mathematical concepts and the language of math. She continually tinkered with how she assigned students to groups to make sure they functioned optimally, given students' changing dispositions and abilities.

Attending to group dynamics. Mary provided plenty of "on the rug" time for the whole class to learn concretely how to support each other in groups. She taught students how to give each other "wait time"; to make sure everyone had a fair number of chances to take the floor; to rephrase contributions to make sure they were understood by everyone; and to use certain phrases to express disagreement with one another respectfully (e.g., "I see what you mean, but here is another way to think about it" rather than "no, you're wrong" or "that's stupid").

Using oral language to support reading and writing. Mary allowed students to "talk and draw" their way through complex math problems before they started to write their answers on paper. In doing so, she encouraged students to use their home language and artistic abilities as stepping stones on the way to understanding and using math vocabulary words, sentence structures, and organizational schemes.

Modeling and providing explicit instruction in language. Mary taught students how to dissect or "tag" the parts of the "show your thinking" word problems by modeling different ways of getting started and teaching students to recognize and use specific action words (e.g., "label," "number," "describe," "explain," "list," "draw," and "give evidence").

Creating a math "word wall." In the context of teaching students to "tag" word problems, she asked them to keep an inventory of important math words (e.g., "numerator," "denominator," "digit") and words and phrases that signaled different kinds of mathematical operations (e.g., "sum," "divided by," and "divided into"). She created a math "word wall" using the language they identified as crucial to doing math. Students used this "word wall" as a resource when they were working independently.

Figure 1. Sample of Marisol's work at the beginning of the school year

Using the writing process. She asked students to draft and revise their math work following the same processes they used in their language arts activities. Mary asked students to share drafts and respond to each others' ideas using guides, graphic organizers, and various worksheets. Next, she asked them to make revisions based on feedback they received from each other and from her in one-on-one conferences. Last, she asked them to proofread their work before turning in final copies.

MARISOL: A CASE STUDY IN THE RESULTS OF MARY'S NEW APPROACHES

To illustrate the changes we observed in Mary's class following the implementation of her language arts–based approaches, Figures 1 and 2 show representative samples of Marisol's "show your thinking" math work and Mary's analyses of these samples. (Mary and Drew focused on Marisol because they found her to be representative of the way many ELL students sometimes struggle with math.)

Marisol wrote the first sample in September (see Figure 1). For this assignment, she was asked to illustrate her understanding of the communicative property of addition (i.e., to explain why it didn't matter in what order she added the numbers in a list). In analyzing Marisol's work, Mary observed:

> Marisol showed no strategies for how she combined the numbers. She copied the number strings and wrote the answers. She did not show or label which numbers she combined to tell how she found the totals. She did not use any of the math vocabulary we talked about. She did, however, make a good attempt to describe what she noticed. She used the words "all around" to explain that the numbers were in mixed-up order. She also tried to let me know that no matter what order the numbers were in, the sum would be the same ("they anyway the disam number 40").

In the next sample from the middle of the year (see Figure 2), Marisol was supposed to read a math problem involving butterflies, show how she solved the problem in graphic form, and explain her approach to the problem in a narrative. In response to Marisol's second sample, Mary noted:

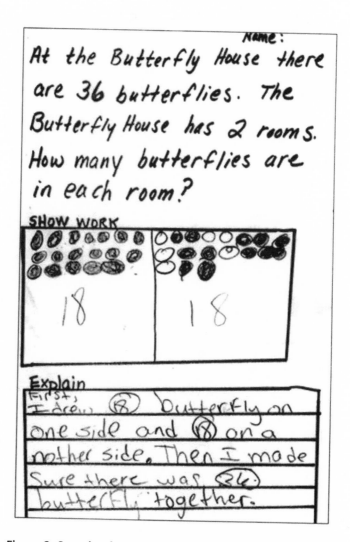

Figure 2. Sample of Marisol's work at mid-year

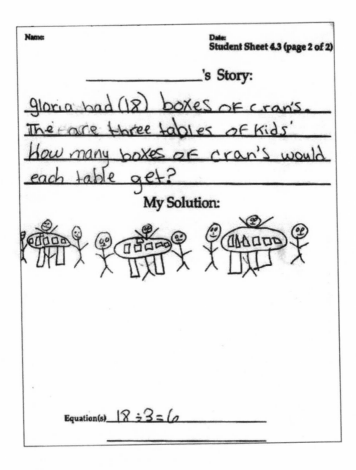

Figure 3. Sample of Marisol's work at the end of the school year

Marisol has begun to organize her thoughts in expected ways. Through her use of "first," "then," and "finally," she seems able to put her actions in order. . . . Her mathematical thinking is still floating at the surface, but she is finally beginning to write the numbers she is using. She can explain that she counted by 4's. I wish that she had explained to me how she knew to put 18 butterflies in each box. . . . Her progress is slow, but she is showing some of the features I had hoped for. One of the most positive outcomes I see is that Marisol is consistent. Once she begins to add these features, she owns them.

Last, in a sample collected at the end of the year, Mary asked students to make up their own word problems and solve them using the procedures and language practices they had been working on all year (see Figure 3). In response to Marisol's spring sample, Mary wrote:

What kind of an impact has all of this teaching had on Marisol, my self-proclaimed hater of math? Last week I gave out math papers for homework. I asked the students to make up their own division story problems, illustrate them, and write a math equation representing their word problem. . . . Marisol came up to my table at dismissal and asked for a bunch of extra papers so she could make-up *extra* math division stories for homework.

LOOKING AHEAD

Our analysis of Marisol's math work and Mary's research notes over the 2003–2004 academic year show how changes in instructional practices supported this student in "owning the language of math" and in shifting from a "self-proclaimed hater of math" to being the kind of student who asks for extra math homework. We believe that Mary's ability to identify and teach the language of math in a meaningful and explicit way contributed to the gains Marisol made.

As the three of us continue to collaborate, we are interested in testing this hypothesis using both qualitative and quantitative measures. We are also interested in designing curriculum and instructional practices that not only apprentice students to the literacy skills they need to play (and win) high-stakes "math games," but also to explore and challenge many of the problems facing linguistically diverse schoolchildren, their families, and their teachers. Just as Mary's new language arts–based approaches represent an interdisciplinary approach to teaching math, why not break disciplinary barriers further and focus students' math work on important school and community issues, such as school funding, attendance figures, and graduation rates among ELL and other student groups? In this way, students can simultaneously learn and use the language of math *and* use their newfound knowledge to accomplish important, real-world work.

CHAPTER 4

Trapezoids, Estuaries, and Kudzu

What English-Language Learners Face on High-Stakes Tests—and How Educators Can Help

Mary T. Jeannot

Regardless of one's opinion on the subject—and everyone seems to have one—high-stakes tests do not appear to be going away any time soon. With $330 million a year spent nationally on tests and the accountability systems surrounding them, the stakes are higher than they have ever been. Nineteen states now require high school exit exams for graduation, and five more states are expected to have their tests in place by 2008.

These tests are often influenced and sometimes even designed by anonymous "outsiders"—some might say business people and politicians dissatisfied with the quality of applicants entering the work force—and the scores received on them are often released as public documents, thus having an impact on students, teachers, administrators, parents, and families. These tests are used to quantify, observe, normalize, standardize, classify, punish, and judge. Never in U.S. history has an educational "reform" (or as the school superintendent of Washington State would prefer to call it, "refocus") caused such controversy.

Criticism and complaints have sprung up in both the popular and academic presses, and on countless websites. They have taken the form of boycotts, protests, legislative action, special commissions, even litigation. Many of these complaints, naturally, have been lodged by the teachers who spend huge portions of their days, especially in the spring, preparing their students for these tests, which often interrupt a school's regular curriculum for two full weeks. A large number of these complaints have also come from teachers whose "underperforming" students bring down a school or district's average scores. These are often teachers who work with "special" populations, English-language learners (ELLs) among them.

WHAT IS BEING TESTED?

As the concerns raised by many English as a Second Language (ESL) teachers illustrate, standardized tests can pose special challenges to ELLs, and these challenges aren't limited to the language arts sections of the test. One illustrative example comes from a tenth-grade science teacher who (relatively speaking) diplomatically complains about the "concept layering" evident within a series of test items on the Washington Assessment of Student Learning (WASL), Washington State's standardized testing system: "When considering a question aimed at graphic interpretation skills, students are asked to consider a scenario involving the salinity of an estuary, the biomass of spartina, and the impact an insect (a cordgrass leafhopper) might have on the situation" (Washington Education Association, 2003).

As this teacher aptly observes, there are a great many concepts embedded in this one question. Estuaries are already an obscure concept to most ELLs, and the question is only made more complicated by the notion of biomass and its relationship to an invasive insect, which also happens to have a rather obscure name. Students are therefore not really being assessed on their thinking processes or their ability to engage in scientific inquiry; instead, they are being tested on their knowledge of (i.e., their ability to memorize) a lot of words.

The same problem is found on the math portions of the WASL. One can only imagine how frustrating the following test questions might be for a gifted Russian or Vietnamese math student who has outperformed his peers in a task-based classroom, but has limited English vocabulary skills and therefore performs less well in his language arts class:

Which of the following statements always describes a trapezoid?

a. A trapezoid has one pair of parallel sides.
b. A trapezoid has one pair of congruent angles.
c. A trapezoid has two pairs of congruent angles.
d. A trapezoid has two pairs of perpendicular sides.

This example illustrates the potential for words to obfuscate the intended message. (It would be far easier for a student to identify a trapezoid from a series of pictures.)

While cross-disciplinary literacy has been the impetus for providing "real-life" scenarios in math, science, and other subject areas, it has also transformed good, old-fashioned story problems on tests into a living hell for ELLs. While they may recognize universal symbols and be able to perform mathematical functions, they now also need to be able to recognize some of the fancy "packaging" around the problems. These kinds of questions have a tendency to measure a student's reading ability or cultural knowledge, not math skills. Further, students are not allowed to use dictionaries for the math and science portions of the test, which simply adds to their stress. Dictionaries are reserved for the writing and reading portions, even though reading and writing are supposed to occur seamlessly across the curriculum.

We all know students who have a low tolerance for ambiguity when reading a difficult passage. The following question appears in an integrated math textbook used to prepare students for the WASL:

> If kudzu really grew a mile a minute, how much would it grow in an hour? (Rubenstein, Craine, & Butts, 1998)

Many students, especially those trained in logographic writing and reading systems (non-alphabetic systems such as Chinese), get irretrievably stuck on the word "kudzu," and since they are prohibited from using dictionaries, they cannot demonstrate what might otherwise be mathematical competence. Moreover, many students from these same cultures are not expected to "show off" their metacognitive abilities (e.g., how one arrives at the answer), so they are unaccustomed to—and often have difficulty—showing the reasons and thought processes behind their responses.

A "SINK OR SWIM" APPROACH

Students are not only subjected to fairly arbitrary test items on some state standardized tests; they are often thrust into a long string of testing situations that are frustrating at best and demoralizing at worst. In some parts of Idaho, for example, ELLs (and others) are required to take the Idaho Student Achievement Test (ISAT) three times per year. Additionally, from kindergarten through third grade, students participate in a K-3 "reading indicator" test. Schools that apply for grants often have even more accountability requirements to fulfill. As one Idaho ESL teacher explains, this adds up to a minimum of eight formal tests per year—almost one a month—for her class. Is *this* much accountability really necessary?

There are some provisions made for the widely divergent group of ELLs in Washington State. They are not required to take the WASL during their first school year. During both days of writing, they are permitted to use a dictionary and a thesaurus in print or electronic form (without spell check), in English or in their native language. Students can have a reader to read the mathematics or science assessment items aloud in English.

Still, most ESL teachers will tell you that these accommodations are inadequate and will paraphrase Jim Cummins in a heartbeat: conversational English is not academic English. That is, students learn much more easily the language of their peers; it takes much longer to learn the stuff of books and school. Another fact well known by now (at least by ESL teachers): strategies, skills, knowledge, and habits transfer from an L1 (first-year English learner) to an L2 (second-year student). If a student is familiar with academic content and culture in her L1 year (how to read, how to take tests, how to make a mind map, how to "be a student") and has uninterrupted schooling prior to immigrating to the United States, chances are she will survive most American schooling contexts and, in time, perform well on tests.

People (teachers included) have less knowledge about and are less prepared to teach or even cope with those students without basic literacy and with little or no prior schooling experience. For the most part, U.S. public schools are ill equipped to deal with this increasingly visible student population who come from poor, rural, or war-torn regions of the world. In short, there is no such thing as a one-size-fits-all set of accommodations.

IMPROVING SUCCESS RATES

Although many educators appear to be aware of the problems that state standardized tests pose for ELLs, change has been slow at the policy level; therefore, many of the problems outlined above will not be solved easily or overnight. Still, in the absence of more widespread change, schools and communities can at the very least work to be more responsive to the ELLs in their own classrooms. Following are a few things educators can do to help their ELLs become better test-takers and—much more importantly—successful and confident learners:

Provide linguistic and cultural support. One of the most difficult ideas for monolingual, monocultural English speakers to grasp is that being supportive of an ELL's language and culture goes beyond learning a few words in their language of origin or sampling their "ethnic" foods. While this may seem obvious to those of us who have experience working with second-language learners, it is not always obvious to mainstream classroom teachers. I have been in many K–12 classrooms in the United States where, in a class of 25 students, there is little to suggest that there are three Belarussians, two Koreans, one Kenyan, and a new brother and sister from Iraq in the class.

Supportive, caring environments are not going to guarantee success on a state test, but they go a long way toward students feeling as if they belong to a community of learners.

School personnel should do everything possible to acknowledge and accommodate ELLs and their families in their native languages. For example, Seattle Public School officials have printed a "Welcome to Our School" poster in 23 languages. They also have partnered with Washington EduPortal, a Seattle Public Schools intranet service made available to school personnel, to create documents in multiple languages for school staff to use in the dissemination of information on such topics as health, the school administration, the National School Lunch Program, and special services.

Where there are resources and when it is possible, schools should make every effort to develop assessment instruments in students' home languages, and both students and their parents or guardians should be interviewed in their home languages to assess prior literacy and other skills. There is ample research to show that the more familiar the school is with a student's linguistic and cultural background, the more successful the student will be. There are some excellent resources for orienting and including families in school cultures, many of them available online. (For example, see the Illinois State Board of Education's homepage: http://www.isbe.net.)

Finally, research has begun to show that systematic, well-conceived bilingual dual-instruction programs can be effective in increasing test scores where there is a preponderance of one group of second-language learners. Describing one such bilingual education program in Washington State, the state school superintendent, in her May 2004 online Progress Report, writes:

At Thompson Elementary School in Grandview, learning is taking place in two languages. Pre-schoolers are learning their ABCs and numbers in both Spanish and English, and older students are becoming fluent and doing schoolwork in both languages. Even though there's a waiting list to get into this innovative dual-language program, the achievement levels of *all* students are rising thanks to the energy and enthusiasm for learning this new program has unleashed in the school (Office of Superintendent of Public Instruction, 2004).

Familiarize students with the academic metalanguage found on the tests. Even ELLs with strong English-language skills can get thrown by some of the language that tends to come up on assessments. Teachers of ELLs should therefore target key test vocabulary and make it part of the daily routine. For example, students should not be surprised on the day of the test by words like "summarize," "explain," "discuss," and "analyze." As seasoned ESL teachers Joan Johnston and Judi Migliazzo explain, "*Compare* and *contrast* are terms found in all parts of standardized testing: math, science, literature, social studies. So, [we] have the students do some sort of compare/contrast paper on a weekly basis." Overlapping strategies and connecting concepts in this way not only helps students succeed on the tests, but carries over and helps them to succeed in a variety of subject areas.

Practice the tests and the questions. Despite what one might believe about standardized tests, few would deny that they can be intimidating to ELLs. It is therefore important to give students a lot of practice taking sample tests in small doses across several content areas, "previewing" some of the specific types of test items they might encounter. In other words, test preparation should be an ongoing activity, part of regular classroom instruction, and integrated into all subject areas. If students are equipped with a variety of test-taking skills and strategies, they are more likely to be comfortable demonstrating their knowledge on a test and less likely to be intimidated by unfamiliar terms. Students should also be familiar with the many different test-item formats. Teachers can help their ELL students in this regard by integrating multiple-choice items, analogies, charts and graphs, and open-ended essay questions into their own lessons, tests, and quizzes.

Use visual aids for test prep. ESL teachers are well known for their creative use of visual aids. The same approaches can be used by all teachers to help prepare students for standardized tests. Teachers should consistently use graphic organizers in presenting material and have students use them as well. Even for ELLs who are not yet proficient writers in English, if they can express their ideas and demonstrate their understanding in an organized table, chart, or outline, they can sometimes gain valuable points on state tests, especially on math questions.

One of the side benefits of using and encouraging the use of graphic organizers is that these tools help to develop students' cognitive abilities in the areas of organization, visualization, and problem-solving. Younger children should be encouraged to verbalize with pictures. Since many tests require students to show their thought processes in either words, numbers, or pictures, many teachers have their ELLs draw pictures throughout the year to "show" what they are thinking. On many state-mandated tests, students are not penalized for showing solutions with pictures. In the words of one ESL teacher, "a good picture speaks a thousand words."

Use systematic writing strategies. Some teachers have experienced success using a systematic approach to writing. One of these techniques, known as Power Writing, has made an enormous difference in how at least one teacher's ELL students score on state tests. Although Power Writing is somewhat controversial, ESL middle school teacher Joan Johnston contends that the approach has helped her students not just on the writing section, but on other areas of the test as well, and that her students' writing now shows the kind of organization and sequencing that is understood by native English speakers and readers—that is, test evaluators.

In order for teachers to help their students produce the kind of writing that will be scored favorably on standardized tests, it is important for them to understand that there are various rhetorical patterns and structures of meaning-making that exist in different languages and cultures. Most native writers of English are trained to develop "reader-friendly" habits that are linear and highly controlled. Depending on her language and culture of origin, such expectations for writing might be confusing to an ELL, who may be accustomed to rhetorical styles that are ambiguous, or what might appear to an English writer as overly inductive. Power Writing is one way to break writing down into manageable chunks. Some teachers argue that this kind of "formulaic" approach stifles creativity, leaving little room for brainstorming and genre exploration and placing too much emphasis on form and method. Notwithstanding its prescriptive nature, ESL teachers consistently report that Power Writing provides students with a system of organization for their writing and a valuable tool to communicate their creative ideas to others more clearly. For good or ill, on many high-stakes tests, "clear" communication and organization of ideas is precisely what "counts."

The purpose of this chapter has been to outline some of the contradictions, paradoxes, and challenges communities face in these high-stakes times that promise to leave no child behind—and to offer a handful of approaches to help make that lofty goal a reality for ELLs. It is important to keep in mind that, in the end, many standardized tests are attempting to measure some things that, in fact, should be measured—but it is also important to remember that some things cannot and should not be measured. With this in mind, I offer elementary teacher Stephen Kramer from Brush Prairie, Washington, the last word. A poster in his classroom displayed next to a list of the state standards reminds him and his students of what genuine accountability is:

1. Learning should be rooted in joy.
2. The most important thing to learn about reading is to love it.
3. We all need help with our writing.
4. For some of us, art and music are as important as breathing.
5. No lesson on math, reading, or writing is so important it can't be interrupted for a lesson on honesty, generosity, or compassion (Matthews, 2004).

REFERENCES

Mathews, J. (2004, June 1). Superintendent debate: Do we need big tests? *Washington Post.*

Office of Superintendent of Public Instruction. (2004). *2004 progress report*. Retrieved August 9, 2004, from www.k12.wa.us/communications/progressreport/may2004.doc.

Rubenstein, R., Craine, T., & Butts, T. (1998). *Integrated mathematics 1*. Evanston, IL: McDougal Littell.

Washington Education Association. (2003). *Teacher comments on Washington Assessment of Student Learning (WASL) 10th grade science test*. Retrieved August 9, 2004, from www.washingtonea.org/member/profdev/accountability/waslscisvy/comments10th.pdf.

FOR FURTHER INFORMATION

J. Bell Kiester. *Blowing Away the State Writing Assessment Test*. Gainesville, FL: Maupin House, 2000.

K. Escamillia, E. Mahon, H. Riley-Bernal, and D. Rutledge. "High Stakes Testing, Latinos and English Language Learners: Lessons from Colorado." *Bilingual Research Journal* 27, no. 1 (2003).

B. Johns. *Eight Tips to Prepare Students for High-Stakes Tests*. Available online at http://www.state.ky.us/agencies/behave/academic/testtips.html

Preparing Your Elementary Students to Take Standardize Tests. Instructional Intranet, Chicago Public Schools. Available online at http://intranet.cps.k12.il.us/Assessments/Preparation/preparation.html.

Preparing Your Secondary Students to Take Standardized Tests. Instructional Intranet, Chicago Public Schools. Available online at http://intranet.cps.k12.il.us/Assessments/Preparation/preparation.html.

P. Shaw. "Leadership in the Diverse School," in *Multilingual Education in Practice*, ed. S. Schecter and J. Cummins. Portsmouth, NH: Heinemann, 2003.

CHAPTER 5

Nurturing "The Writer's Voice"

Helping Students Construct a Self in a New Language and Culture

Greta Vollmer

> As a writer, I have strong feelings and thinking that are a part of me, and I want those things reflected in my writing so the reader can have a sense of me. If you don't express it very well, people might not get it, so . . . for me, it's important people get it.[*]
>
> —*Leah, eleventh-grade English-language learner*

Developing as a writer is often seen as one of the most difficult and complex tasks for a second-language learner. While research on second-language writing has expanded dramatically in recent years, researchers have for the most part considered writing either a learner's mental activity (i.e., the learner's composing processes or strategies) or the text itself. Increasingly, though, researchers

---

[*]Passages from student writing are included exactly as written.

have taken a keen interest in the role of culture and identity in second-language learning, and as a result have developed what is known as a sociocultural theory of language acquisition (see, e.g., Kern, 2000; Kramsch, 2000; Lantolf, 2000). From this sociocultural perspective, writing is not merely situated within the individual learner; it is also a function of the social context in which students write and learn.

THE WRITER'S VOICE: CONSTRUCTING A SELF

If we understand the expression of identity to be an essential component of writing, we must then look carefully at written texts as evidence of participation in a given culture. How do second-language writers position themselves in these texts, and what linguistic and rhetorical resources do they use to do so? In the first-person narratives of bilingual authors such as Eva Hoffman (1989) and Andre Codrescu (1990), researchers Aneta Pavlenko and James Lantolf (2000) find a rich source of evidence for the ways in which language learners both lose and reconstruct their identities in a second language. The authors delineate the stages of initial loss, which include a loss of linguistic identity, a loss of the "inner voice," and a loss of the first language. In her memoir, *Lost in Translation: A Life in a New Language*, Hoffman offers one of the more eloquent descriptions of this linguistic journey:

> I wait for that spontaneous flow of inner language which used to be my nighttime talk with myself. Nothing comes. Polish, in a short time, has atrophied, shriveled from sheer uselessness. Its words don't apply to my new experiences; they're not coeval with any of the objects, or faces, or the very air I breathe in the daytime. In English, the words have

not penetrated to those layers of my psyche from which a private connection could be processed. (cited in Pavlenko & Lantolf, 2000, p. 165)

As with the loss of voice, recovery of voice also has multiple stages. Two of these—the appropriation of other voices and the emergence of one's new voice—seem particularly evident in the work of second-language writers. They may "try on" new language and voices, borrowed from spoken English or written texts, to augment their own emerging voices.

One need not look only to accomplished adult writers to document the evolving representation of self in second-language writing. Leah, the eleventh grader quoted above, was one such writer, whose development I observed over the course of a year I spent as a researcher in ESL classrooms focused on writing. In Leah's class, students were free to develop their own "creations," either poetry or prose. Leah was an independent yet sometimes demanding student whose teacher spoke of her with both affection and exasperation. Leah would often seek me out for conferences on her writing when the teacher was busy with others. In this essay, Leah chose to write eloquently about her own "changing reality":

When I left my country I thought all the things I have mention will go away, but the life I've left behind will remain the same. . . . I was living in the upper classes of Ethiopia . . . I was privelaged in a lot of things.

Leah then recounts her first attempt to get a job because, as she explains it, "I got the impression that teenagers in America are expected to take care of themselves in certain levels." Leah's attempts to get work and find a place for herself are frustrating to her, and she observes that she is "completely mystified about what the future and America holds for me, [and] I find myself sluggish in the reality of living."

In Leah's writing, and in subsequent conversations I had with her, it was clear to me that she was negotiating the currents of changing circumstances and identities and trying to make sense of these in her writing: a protected upper-class child, and now an independent working teenager; an Ethiopian who misses her birthplace but speaks of the "dark reality of the third world country." In the same essay, she identifies as an immigrant yet distances herself from "most immigrants who come here [thinking America] is heaven." She does not accept that she must become "American," yet acknowledges that she cannot remain as she was in Ethiopia either. She sees herself as both an insider and an outsider.

In our conversations, it was also clear that Leah was aware of the evolution in her own perspective and sense of identity, changes she jokingly referred to as "the before and after Leah." Sadly, Leah felt overwhelmed by the task she had taken on in this essay and ultimately abandoned it. Yet researchers have found that such writing, rich in interrogation and exploration, represents the potential for the young second-language writer to "reconstruct a self" in a new social context.

THE WRITING CLASSROOM: THE CONSTRUCTED SELF

Typically, second-language writers have been viewed from a deficit perspective, whereby educators see them as developmentally weak and their writing as deficient and riddled with language errors. Understanding second-language writing as active participation in the construction of a "discourse identity" offers a very different view of these same writers, as with Leah. But just as writers construct themselves textually, sociocultural linguists point out that the context in turn constructs the writer. Researcher Linda Harklau (2000) offers a vivid illustration of how one group of second-language learners were viewed in radically different ways as they moved from high school to a community college context. Seen as the "good kids" in high school, they were viewed as problematic and difficult when placed in ESL classrooms at the community college, where they did not fit the "recently arrived immigrant" identity that was presumed for these students. This shift in external perceptions had a very negative impact on the students' academic performance (including their writing) and on their motivation to learn.

In my own research with second-language writers, I found that some teachers followed a writing workshop approach with these students and offered them a "free choice" from selected composition topics. Upon delving deeper, however, I discovered that these same teachers restrained and constricted their students' writing by offering them only topics related to their immigrant identities. For example, in one ESL classroom I observed, students were assigned the topic, "My Definition of Success." All the classroom discussion and readings leading up to this assignment, however, focused on and reinforced the standard "immigrant success story"—attributed to hard work and sacrifice—with which we are all familiar. Students in this class produced cookie-cutter essays that echoed this classic immigrant success story and showed little evidence of investment or personal voice in their work.

These cases speak to the need to recognize not only the ways student writers seek to construct a new identity—and multiple identities—in a second language, but also the ways classroom practices and assignments may assume and rein-force narrowly defined identities for these writers (Vollmer, 2000).

IMPLICATIONS FOR TEACHING SECOND-LANGUAGE WRITING

What does this mean for teachers of writing? Clearly, we must acknowledge the slipperiness of some of the concepts set forth by sociocultural theory. There is no easy agreement on what is meant by social identity, the self, or even culture. Yet we also know—and sociocultural theory confirms this—that writing is a powerful tool with which second-language writers can explore multiple facets of their lives—and multiple iden-tities. Immigrant students often are content to (and at times are encouraged to) write on "safe" topics, producing simple "my country" descriptions or recounting their "how I came to America" narrative over and over again. Can we instead encourage our immigrant students to explore in writing the cultural fault lines they are navigating, to be comfortable with the shifting perspectives they will undoubtedly have on their new lives? While acknowledging that "writing from what you know" is a powerful creative force, it is important for us to en-courage our students to write about what they are less certain of, perhaps what they don't know they know, at least not yet.

In Leah's class, I observed one peer exchange that illus-trates the richness that can be lost if we allow students' deeper knowledge of themselves, their cultures, and their own experiences both here and in their countries of origin to go untapped. In this instance Tran, a Vietnamese student, had composed her version of a Vietnamese legend in which a young woman disobeys her father, eats a forbidden peach from a sacred garden, and becomes pregnant as a result. As part of a peer response assignment, Tran offered her composition, "The God Peach Story," to Tsega, an Ethiopian classmate, for comments. Tsega responded carefully and at length, offering her suggested changes to Tran's story as follows:

> Their names were Adam and Eve. Their God told Adam not to eat the fruit (maybe peach but I don't remember what kind of fruit). The snake tells Adam and Eve to eat the fruit. God was sad, and then Adam regret why he broke his promise.

The following day, the two writers engaged in a lively discussion of the tale. Tsega was enthusiastic: "I think it's true. I think it's history. It's a Bible story." Then she added earnestly, "If you were a Christian, you could write this really good." With a spirited grin, Tran responded, "I don't want no God in there!"

The teacher gently intervened: "Tsega, you must not feel offended that Tran is going to reject your suggestions and keep the story Buddhist." As the teacher moved away, Tsega added apologetically, "I had to say something." Tran nodded and returned to her paper, simply saying, "That's OK." Her subsequent revisions focused on spelling and grammar, but she made few other changes.

In this exchange, we see that two cultural perspectives approached each other but were ultimately left unexplored. What might have happened instead? Perhaps as teachers we need not steer clear of such cultural fault lines, but instead use our students' writing as a tool for entering a third place, where writers can take both an insider's and an outsider's view of their culture. (Kramsch, 1993). Tran and Tsega could have explored more thoroughly the similarities and differences of their versions. As writers seeing through the eyes of the other, they could have perhaps reached a negotiated understanding not only of each other's versions of the tale, but also of the deeper cultural value such stories hold.

Learners can use their writing to question and explore representations of culture (their own and others') or to question their role as narrator/author in a new cultural context. In this sense, second-language writers become what researcher Claire Kramsch calls "border crossers." This journey is never easy, as Hoffman and many others have illustrated. As Kramsch (1993) notes, "The realization of difference, not only between oneself and others, but between one's personal and one's social self, indeed between different perceptions of oneself, can be at once an elating and deeply troubling experience" (p. 234).

But if we understand writing as a medium through which language learners attempt to understand and control the shifting perspectives in their lives, to express and explore new identities, and to represent themselves in new ways in a new cultural context, writing in a second language can become a powerfully motivating and potentially transformative force. For writers like Leah, Tran, and Tsega, this could mean more opportunities to communicate a sense of themselves, as well as a greater understanding of the linguistic and cultural resources they have to explore those opportunities.

This chapter is adapted from "Sociocultural Perspectives on Second Language Writing," which appeared in the news bulletin of the ERIC Clearinghouse on Languages and Linguistics and the Center for Applied Linguistics in Spring 2002. Available online at http://www.cal.org/resources/news.

REFERENCES

Codrescu, A. (1990). *The disappearance of the outside: A manifesto for escape.* Boston: Addison-Wesley.

Harklau, L. (2000). From the "good kids" to the "worst": Representations of English language learners across educational settings. *TESOL Quarterly, 34,* 35–67.

Hoffman, E. (1989). *Lost in translation: A life in a new language.* New York: Dutton.

Kern, R. (2000). *Literacy and language teaching.* New York: Oxford University Press.

Kramsch, C. (1993). *Context and culture in language teaching.* New York: Oxford University Press.

Kramsch, C. (2000). Social discursive constructions of self in L2 learning. In J. Lantolf (Ed.), *Sociocultural theory and second language learning* (pp. 133–153). New York: Oxford University Press.

Lantolf, J. (2000). *Sociocultural theory and second language learning.* New York: Oxford University Press.

Pavlenko, A., & Lantolf, J. (2000). Second language learning as participation and the (re)construction of selves. In J. Lantolf (Ed.), *Sociocultural theory and second language learning* (pp. 155–177). New York: Oxford University Press.

Vollmer, G. (2000). *Classroom contexts for academic literacy: The intersection of language and writing development in secondary ESL classrooms.* Unpublished doctoral dissertation, University of California, Berkeley.

CHAPTER 6

How Schools Can Help Refugee Students

Shaun Sutner

Johnny Brewch, a stocky 15-year-old with a quick smile and a tangle of silver chains around his neck, tries to concentrate as his teacher writes President Franklin D. Roosevelt's name on the blackboard. Most of the students in Johnny's social studies class at the Nathan Bishop Middle School in Providence, Rhode Island, jot the words in their notebooks. But the eighth grader fidgets, impulsively hopping in and out of his chair.

After fleeing a brutal civil war in his native Liberia, Johnny struggles in a school system that is underequipped to deal with him and the thousands of refugees who have settled here in recent years. In addition to newcomers' typical challenges—grasping a strange language, fitting into new social circles, and learning a different culture's customs—refugee children often contend with a host of psychological problems.

Johnny still remembers seeing people killed in the street. "Sometimes when I sit and think, it bothers me," he says in his thickly accented English. "I dream about how they killed. I dream how they cut people's hands off."

Because they have often witnessed terrible violence, many refugee students suffer from post-traumatic stress disorder (PTSD), a condition that can produce flashbacks, sleep disorders, depression, and emotional numbing. Statistically, they also are more likely to join gangs and abuse drugs and alcohol. Many have arrived from places like Afghanistan and Somalia having lost one or both parents, and they frequently face problems at home, including physical abuse.

Since the September 11, 2001, terrorist attacks and the numerous deadly school shootings of the 1990s, many schools are waking up to PTSD's impact on students, and that awareness has expanded to include refugees, experts say. But because teachers are not typically trained to recognize such symptoms and funding for intervention is scarce, many children with PTSD may not get the attention or treatments they need, such as psychotherapy and antidepressant drugs.

"Children who come here who are displaced already faced stressful problems in their own countries, and the displacement adds significant stress," says Syed Arshad Husain, professor of child psychiatry at the University of Missouri–Columbia. "Psychological treatment is [what's] least available but most needed."

Husain's study of Bosnian adolescents who survived the siege of Sarajevo in 1994 showed that experiencing warfare and the death of loved ones was likely to produce PTSD in children. Bosnian girls were more likely to develop symptoms than boys, says Husain. He suggests three possible reasons why: the girls tended to internalize their feelings more than boys did; they were more socially sheltered in a macho culture before the war and therefore more traumatized by the outbreak of violence; and that particular war sparked daily fear of sexual assault.

MORE THAN BILINGUAL EDUCATION

School administrators are learning that effectively teaching refugee students usually entails more than simply placing them in bilingual education programs. In working-class Chelsea, Massachusetts, many students come from places of war or famine. (About 20 percent of the district's 5,600-plus students are classified as limited English proficient.) In recent years, the district has added social workers from such countries as Somalia and Bosnia and has begun providing grant-funded, intensive English literacy and math instruction for refugee students before transferring them to bilingual classes.

After years of welcoming students from 50 different countries into her classroom, Linda Quinn, the high school's lead bilingual teacher, believes she knows how to spot traumatized refugees. "Some are very silent. They can be very angry. They'll sit in back and not mix with other kids in the cafeteria," she says.

In struggling urban school systems like Chelsea or Providence, crowded classes and high student mobility make it hard for teachers to give enough attention to individual children. Refugee agencies in Providence focus mainly on resettling new arrivals, with little time or money to attend to educational issues. "It's been a nightmare to get any special help for these kids," says Betty Simons, director of refugee services for the International Institute of Providence. "The schools just are not prepared and don't have the resources. It's an ongoing struggle." Sharon O'Neill, who teaches English as a Second Language, concurs: "They arrive here and they're dumped in a class with 28 kids."

To aid schools, the federal government has provided funds to address the issue of students with PTSD. The National Child Traumatic Stress Initiative was launched in 2001 by the U.S. Department of Health and Human Services and has distributed more than $30 million over three years to research and clinical treatment centers across the country. Boston Medical Center and Boston University School of Medicine were awarded $1.8 million under the initiative to research and treat posttraumatic stress in refugee children and help schools deal with the problem.

The Boston partnership team is made up of ten psychiatrists, psychologists, and social workers who offer therapy and home visits to the families of refugee children. The children they see often "have experienced unbelievable trauma, some of the worst we've seen—torture, physical abuse, rapes," says Glen Saxe, chairman of child and adolescent psychiatry at Boston Medical Center. "[These children] may show aggressive behavior and [have] a great deal of difficulty focusing in school because they're processing very frightening memories, and teachers may not recognize that."

Team members instruct teachers to find out more about students' backgrounds, and how certain classroom factors can trigger traumatic memories. Interpreters from the hospital staff provide critical help in this work. For example, roughhousing in the classroom or schoolyard can be upsetting to children who have experienced intense violence, Saxe says. "Teachers may not know that speaking in a certain tone of voice that is highly reminiscent of what they've gone though can trigger bad memories," he says. "Some have witnessed assault by someone in the military, and they may be mistrustful of anyone in authority."

Indeed, many teachers have realized on their own that they need to know more about how to teach the newcomers who end up in their classrooms. With some 75,000 refugees arriving in the United States each year, school systems are starting to routinely prepare teachers to handle refugees from the new conflict zones that emerge around the globe.

In the Miami-Dade County public schools, Project Flourish is using a $600,000 federal grant for training teachers to help youths who were caught up in the murderous guerilla war in Colombia and others who left poverty and civil strife in Haiti. Weekend training conferences have proved popular, with 100 teachers showing up for recent sessions.

Teachers are shown how students' ability to learn is often inextricably linked to what they went though in their flight from their home country. "They need to understand where the kids come from and what kind of history they have. Why are they here?" says Mercy Suarez, the project's manager. She says teachers should invite students to tell their stories: Who did they leave behind? What has the journey been like? "People think that if you don't talk about it, they'll forget," says Suarez. "But when you have a trauma, you need to talk about it."

LONG-LASTING EFFECTS

Educators should know that displaced trauma can be long lasting, says James Garbarino, a Cornell University researcher who studies the impact of violence on children. In a study of Cambodian and Khmer children, Garbarino found that half of his sample group showed signs of posttraumatic stress even after ten years in the United States. One way to treat the disorder is to involve youths in community projects such as gardening or taking care of animals, he says: "Particularly with chronic stress, it's not enough to treat them clinically. Sometimes you have to restore their faith in the future."

Many children thrust into U.S. schools after surviving mayhem and privation arrive with the added burden of a fragmented or foreshortened formal education. While refugee experiences vary, it is common for displaced children—particularly those from some African countries—to miss out on school or receive a substandard education. In Guinea's Forest Region, where more than 200,000 Liberians fled in the 1990s, refugees were placed in camps far from the capital and reached only by rutted dirt roads. The few schools were poorly equipped, and the language of instruction was generally French, while Liberians are primarily English speaking. In similar camps throughout the world, families are sometimes charged fees for their children's schooling, forcing penniless refugees to somehow come up with money for uniforms, shoes, and school supplies.

The educational quality and customs in refugee camps in developing countries are often much different from those in industrialized nations. In some cultures, schoolchildren are not allowed to speak in class, or must look down and answer quietly out of respect for the adult teacher. "It's one of the big challenges for kids when they come here. Not only are they facing a new language, new environment, and new culture, they are facing a new educational culture," says Hiram A.

Ruiz, spokesman for the Washington, D.C.–based Immigration and Refugee Services of America.

Of course, the range of experiences among refugees is wide. Experts note that the most extreme cases—the students who tune out completely or turn to violence or serious drug abuse—are just that: extreme and still somewhat rare. Although refugees' passage from one world to another is frequently arduous and painful, the transition is often ultimately successful—and a relief.

For example, Aladin Milutinovic escaped Bosnia with his Muslim mother and Eastern Orthodox Christian father when he was ten years old. His father is now Chelsea High School's soccer coach. Having grown up amid civil war, Aladin remembers hearing the gunfire and bombing. "My family came here because of the troubles," says Aladin, now 18 and one of the top students in his graduating class. "I don't dwell on them. I am looking forward to a better future."

Madina Mohamed, a 19-year-old senior at Chelsea High School, is another good example. She left Somalia as a young child, leaving behind a chaotic civil war among rival warlord gangs. During her five years in a refugee camp in Kenya she never attended school. Though she speaks English fluently, she reads and writes with difficulty, and her goal of graduating this year and attending college may be unattainable. "If I had been more in school, I would be in college by now," she says. "I had to catch up."

Despite Madina's struggles, she and many of her peers remain highly motivated, says Chelsea High School principal Harold B. Elder Jr. Some have advantages: they come from middle-class, cosmopolitan backgrounds and arrive with both parents. Many Bosnian and Croatian refugees who experienced the war got good schooling in Germany's refugee camps, says Elder. "They realize the value of an education because of what's happened to them."

This chapter originally appeared in the September/October 2002 issue of the *Harvard Education Letter*.

FOR FURTHER INFORMATION

J. Garbarino, K. Kostelny, and N. Dubrow. *No Place to Be a Child: Growing Up in a War Zone.* San Francisco: Jossey-Bass, 1998.

S.J. Grosse. "Children and Post-Traumatic Stress Disorder: What Classroom Teachers Should Know." Washington, DC: ERIC Clearinghouse on Teaching and Teacher Education, 2001 (ERIC Document Reproduction Service No. 2001-01).

S.A. Husain, J. Nair, W. Holcomb, J.C. Reid, V. Vargas, S.S. Nair. "Stress Reactions of Children and Adolescents in War and Siege Conditions." *American Journal of Psychiatry* 155, no. 12 (1998): 1718–1719.

C.D. Johnson and S.K. Johnson. *Building Stronger School Counseling Programs: Bringing Futuristic Approaches into the Present.* Greensboro, NC: ERIC Counseling and Student Services Clearinghouse, 2002.

The National Child Traumatic Stress Initiative of the U.S. Department of Health and Human Services offers advice for talking to students about disasters, as well as program and grant application information. Available online at www.mentalhealth.org/cmhs/emergencyservices/childstress.asp.

Northwest Regional Education Laboratory. *Improving Education for Immigrant Students: A Resource Guide for K–12 Educators in the Northwest and Alaska.* Portland, OR: Author, 1998. Available at www.nwrel.org/cnorse/booklets/immigration/.

The United Nations High Commissioner for Refugees offers resources for teaching about refugees at www.unhcr.ch.

The University of Oxford's Refugee Studies Centre offers a number of resources for teachers of refugees at www.forcedmigration.org/rfgexp.

CHAPTER 7

Teaching Migrant Students

Lessons from Successful Districts

Reino Makkonen

Leonel wants to be an archeologist. He studies hard, aces most of his science quizzes, and always earns straight As—quite an accomplishment for a young man who changes schools several times a year.

Leonel's parents migrate continually between Texas and the Midwest (Michigan and Illinois) to obtain seasonal employment, yet his outstanding fourth-grade achievements at several schools led to Leonel's being named the 2003 Migrant Student of the Year by the National Association of State Directors of Migrant Education.

Migrant farmworkers in the United States typically follow one of three geographic streams on the East Coast, Midwest, or West Coast. On the East Coast, most workers have their primary residence (or "home base") in southern Florida and follow the crops northward to the Mid-Atlantic states, while the majority of West Coast migrant farmworkers depart home bases in Southern California and head north to Idaho, Oregon, or Washington. South Texas is the home base of most Midwestern migrant workers. Overall, there are an estimated 500,000 migrant students in the United States, and more than 116,000 of them (including Leonel) go to school in Texas—the state with the nation's largest migrant population.

Few migrant students are as successful as Leonel, however. Because of the disruptions caused by irregular attendance, language barriers (most migrant students have limited proficiency in academic English), and poverty, most run a high risk of educational failure. But several recent studies have shed light on school districts that have been able to promote educational continuity and academic achievement among this population.

EDUCATIONAL CONTINUITY

In 2002, a U.S. Department of Education (DOE) study identified practices that effectively promote a stable instructional environment for migrant students. After examining successful "partner" schools and districts (those that share migrant populations) in Texas and Washington, Texas and Montana, Florida and Michigan, and California and Arizona, DOE researchers recommended that high-migrant schools and districts work to improve their capacity for information exchange and expand opportunities for supplemental instruction.

Information Exchange

Today's high-quality email and information systems allow districts to transfer migrant students' academic records between partner schools and provide access to another state's or district's assessments and standards. For example, the New

Generation System (NGS) is a web-based interstate information network that has been operated by the Migrant Division of the Texas Education Agency (TEA) since 1995. The system allows educators in 20 states to access and exchange migrant students' academic and health data in real time, thus providing teachers and administrators with up-to-the-minute profiles of their students' backgrounds and needs.

Supplemental Instruction

Successful high-migrant districts often confront the problem of lost instructional time at the secondary level by developing flexible courses of study and delivering additional instructional time in the summer, at night, or during the school day. Flexible courses often take advantage of technology to deliver and individualize instruction, while effective districts also provide additional time for migrant students to complete regular course work, work on their independent courses of study, or prepare for statewide tests.

IDEAS INTO PRACTICE: THE WESLACO INDEPENDENT SCHOOL DISTRICT

Weslaco was recently recognized by the Texas state legislature for its success with migrant students, a group that makes up nearly a third of the district's student population. In Weslaco, migrant students at the elementary and middle school levels work with tutors and study on computers after school, and the district's two high schools provide migrant students with their own "lab," complete with books, academic and tutorial software, and University of Texas correspondence course work. In 2002, 80 percent of Weslaco's migrant students passed statewide exit examinations in reading, math, and writing.

According to Linda Taormina, Weslaco's Title I Migrant Coordinator, the district's success goes beyond specific programs. "From the superintendent on down, we accept no excuses. We're not going to say we don't expect these kids to pass because they're migrants," Taormina says. "I don't go on the campuses telling principals what to do [to help migrant students], but I do say, 'These kids really need the help, what have you got in mind?' And we work together to do what we can."

Indeed, the DOE's 2002 migrant report continually emphasized the importance of committed and prepared personnel in high-migrant districts like Weslaco, noting that much can be achieved through collaboration and creativity. As the researchers noted, "Changes to programs and systems do not occur without staff members who hold the attitude and belief that the outcomes will be better for migrant students if colleagues, schools, districts, and states work together (p. 41)."

Successful Instruction

In a 2003 study of schools with large migrant populations, University of Texas at Austin researchers Pedro Reyes and Carol Fletcher (2003) set out to identify successful instructional strategies for working with migrant students that could be transferred to other schools with large migrant populations. The researchers found that schools with high levels of math achievement among their migrant students focused on teacher collaboration, student reflection, real-world problem-solving, and frequent review.

Reyes and Fletcher first worked with state officials to compile data on school districts where migrant students achieved at a high level. They identified districts with at least an 80 percent graduation rate, an 80 percent promotion rate, and a 94 percent school attendance rate among migrant students. Six districts were selected for the final sample—four in Texas, one in Illinois, and one in Montana. In the selected districts, the researchers sought out schools where at least 70 percent of migrant students passed statewide tests in math, reading, and writing.

"Teachers and principals kept coming back to the fact that they didn't do anything different [for migrant students]," Fletcher says, echoing Taormina's sentiments. "Their purpose was to reach students as individuals, not see them as different groups. It's an attitude of, 'We don't teach these kids as migrants, we teach them as students who need to learn math.'"

According to the University of Texas researchers, four organizational practices stood out as especially successful in high-migrant schools:

- *A workplace focused on instructional improvement.* Teachers in successful schools work together to review students' test scores, set and reflect on goals, and focus on self-evaluation, concentrating their energy on how to teach rather than what to teach. Data guides teaching, but it is merely a tool. "We look forward to meetings," a teacher in the Texas study explained. "Everybody supports each other, and they share with each other."

- *High expectations for all students.* Weslaco's focus on achievement for all students was also common among the successful districts in the University of Texas study. Instead of using unique curriculum or special instructional techniques for migrant students, effective high-migrant schools emphasized high expectations and also worked to bring personal experiences and backgrounds into the classroom environment. "The ultimate philosophy was, 'I'm going to meet the student where he is and give him the support he needs to get where he needs to be,'" Fletcher says.

- *Student-centered instruction focused on problem-solving.* To best teach skills and concepts, teachers in successful high-migrant schools strove to incorporate relevant "real-world" content. Problem-solving and collaboration were taught as life skills, and tangible classroom examples included small groups of students working together to calculate a monthly budget or figure out how much wallpaper is needed to decorate a room. The schools also made use of extensive support systems for students, including peer tutoring workshops and dedicating the last period of the day to tutoring, as in Weslaco.

- *Spiraling curriculum emphasizing constant review.* Teachers in the successful schools would often cover the same math objective four or five times during the school year, requiring students to make connections between key concepts. And both teachers and students built portfolios of their work, fashioning a concrete record of their career and academic achievements.

With effective instructional and organizational strategies like those identified in these recent studies, the challenge now shifts to broader implementation—giving *all* migrant students access to a quality education and the opportunity to overcome the disruptions of migration. It will not be easy. Interstate and district-to-district coordination requires patience, hard work, leadership, commitment, and institutional support. And it takes time and effort for teachers and administrators to build the collaborative structures, attitudes, and relationships that lead to successful migrant student outcomes. For today's high-migrant schools, though, excuses are a diminishing option. As Fletcher observes, "When you see positive results, it creates a positive cycle."

A short article highlighting some of the research cited in this chapter appeared in the January/February 2004 issue of the Harvard Education Letter.

REFERENCES

Reyes, P., & Fletcher, C. (2003). Successful migrant students: The case of mathematics. *Journal of Curriculum and Supervision, 18,* 306–333.

U.S. Department of Education, Office of the Under Secretary. (2002). *Coordinating the education of migrant students: Lessons learned from the field.* Washington, DC: Author.

CHAPTER 8

Raising the Achievement of English-Language Learners

How Principals Can Make a Difference

Maricel G. Santos

According to federal survey data, there are 4.5 million English-language learners (ELLs) enrolled in U.S. public schools (preK–12), roughly twice as many as were enrolled in 1990 (Kindler, 2002). Given this fast-growing number of linguistically and culturally diverse children, principals are dealt an increasingly urgent responsibility: to lead their schools in helping *all* students succeed academically. The federal No Child Left Behind Act (NCLB) requires educators to raise not just the overall achievement of their students, but that of all major student subgroups. Are the nation's school principals ready to rise to this challenge? What must administrators do to improve the academic achievement of young language-minority students and fulfill the requirements of NCLB?

Strong instructional leadership seems to be fundamental. The need to implement standards-based reform is not lost on

Guadalupe Guerrero, a principal at Dever Elementary School in Boston, where approximately one-fourth of the school's 520 students are ELLs from Central and South America, the Caribbean, Cape Verde, Vietnam, Central Asia, Eastern Europe, the Middle East, and Africa. Guerrero carefully monitors his students' performance, looking closely at class work and test scores.

"This enables me to get a complete picture of where students are experiencing success, and where they are not," Guerrero says. "Wherever there seems to be a discrepancy, you need to uncover what the real causes are. This can be a painful discussion—that is, why one group of children is not achieving as well as another group in the same classroom. Sometimes this means the instruction is not meeting the needs of one particular group of students."

Guerrero has worked to implement a coherent plan designed to yield improved academic achievement in a school where more than 20 percent of the students have identified special learning needs. Also, Dever Elementary was recently designated as a center for English-language education, a move that propelled Guerrero to make some hard decisions to improve the quality of instruction. The firing of some bilingual teachers whose English fluency he viewed as inadequate caused many people to feel resentful, he recalls. However, as the school leader, Guerrero says it was essential that he remain "transparent" about his goals.

"I believe that teachers are our most important asset, and I make it a priority to support teachers," he says. "However, when a teacher isn't able to provide effective instruction, then I have to put on another hat and deal with it. I don't walk around with that threat, but it's important to know what kind of instruction is going to meet the needs of the students."

ACTING DECISIVELY

Guerrero's response highlights an undeniable reality: principals must sometimes make difficult decisions in order to make a difference in the education of language-minority students. Carmen Jimenez, director of the Professional Development Leadership Center in the Bronx, New York, agrees that strong, decisive leadership is key to the success of English-language learners. In her professional development work, Jimenez reminds the principals with whom she works that they must stay committed to a vision of academic excellence for all children. For one thing, she exhorts new principals to make sure that they—as well as their teaching staffs—are aware of the ways in which their behavior conveys expectations for ELL student achievement.

For example, suppose a principal walks into an ESL classroom and finds that the teacher has not prepared a coherent lesson plan. Jimenez says, "If you let that go, if you don't go completely nuts over that, you set a new standard, a *low* standard."

Of course, part of being able to make effective changes as a school leader involves what Harvard Graduate School of Education professor Richard Elmore (2003) calls "knowing the right thing to do." In response to reform efforts, school principals are under great pressure to take steps to improve instruction so that all students meet rigorous learning standards. Yet, Elmore says, many are simply expected to know what changes need to be made and to implement those changes. When it comes to raising the achievement of second-language learners, however, many administrators are at a loss for strategies.

How do principals figure out the "right things to do" to educate linguistically and culturally diverse children? Roger

Nyeffler, an elementary school principal in Kearney, Neb., with 25 years' experience, didn't leave things to chance. Instead, he enrolled in a multiculturalism program at the local university to learn about the complex intersection of culture and student learning.

"I knew things were changing . . . and my knowledge [about the newcomer families] was limited," Nyeffler says. A city of about 30,000 residents, Kearney is home to a meat-packing industry that in recent years has drawn an increasing number of immigrants looking for employment. This year the cafeteria at Central Elementary, where Nyeffler is principal, displays 12 flags to represent the students' various countries of birth. Nyeffler also makes sure that the teachers in his school are given professional development opportunities, similar to his own, to learn about the cultures and traditions of the newcomer families.

Greater awareness about the needs of immigrant families has also led Nyeffler to call for more differentiated instruction at Central Elementary. Some teachers have welcomed these changes, Nyeffler says, while others have resisted. But like Guerrero, Nyeffler is clear about his responsibilities as an instructional leader in addressing the needs of the newcomer children. "At some point, you have to get on the bus . . . or get out of the way," he says. "In fact, my role is to help you know where you'll board and where you'll sit. By this I mean I should know how to place teachers where they'll be most effective."

SUPPORTING TEACHERS' GROWTH

In the neighboring state of Colorado, principal Gayle Jones encounters similar issues in preparing her teachers to work effectively with the newcomer children at Dillon Valley Elementary School. In the mid 1990s, the Dillon Valley school district watched its ELL enrollment jump from an average of three students per school to more than 100 in about three years. Today about 43 percent of the children at Dillon Valley Elementary are English-language learners. The children are largely Latino and come from families who moved to the area seeking employment as service workers in the region's upscale ski resorts, such as Vail and Aspen.

Jones observes that the demographic changes in her district at first caused some disequilibrium among her faculty. "It's tough to see excellent teachers suddenly feeling unsuccessful. They doubt their own practice," she notes. "But the teachers who fare best are those who are willing to learn, to accept the changes."

Under Jones' leadership, the district has garnered Title VII money to support professional development, specifically to help teachers earn endorsement as ESL teachers. These funds, Jones says, certainly make her job as an administrator easier. The school was able to train bilingual paraprofessionals to work with classroom teachers and to hire a full-time English-language education coordinator, who offers teachers professional development workshops after school.

Guadalupe Guerrero, Roger Nyeffler, and Gayle Jones are all principals who have made the academic achievement of English-language learners a priority and have taken steps to ensure that instruction is aligned with this goal. While the results of their efforts have been difficult to measure so far, their approach to leadership is one that California State University researcher Claude Goldenberg and teacher Jessie Sullivan have identified as highly effective in improving educational opportunity for ELLs. Co-authors of a 1994 study that profiled a successful effort to raise achievement in a largely Latino Los Angeles–area elementary school, Goldenberg and Sullivan say that school leaders need to provide both "support" and "pressure":

> Although these two [functions] appear to be at odds, we see them as complementary and as producing a creative tension. The skillful principal—indeed, the skillful leader—will know when to exercise one or the other or both simultaneously.

Dillon Valley Elementary principal Jones demonstrates this dual leadership role in her work with teachers who struggle to accept the curricular changes prompted by the area's shifting demographics. She works to reassure the teachers that they are capable of working with a diverse population of children, but she also expects them to participate in professional development and training on the needs of English-language learners.

This characterization of effective leadership stands in stark contrast to the "command and control" image of the principalship that prevails in many schools, say Elizabeth Hale and Hunter Moorman (2003) of the Institute for Educational Leadership in Washington, D.C. Hale and Moorman are critical of many educational leadership programs in higher education that prioritize managerial skills and place relatively little attention on developing instructional leadership competencies. These programs are an especially ill fit, they note, in today's educational context, where principals are expected to raise the achievement levels of a diverse group of learners.

WHO ARE MY ELL STUDENTS?
A SELF-ASSESSMENT FOR PRINCIPALS

Principals can take the first steps toward improving learning opportunities for English-language learners (ELLs) by assessing what they know about these students and the issues that affect them. Following are eight questions to consider if there are ELL students in your school.

1. How much do I know about the English-language learners in my school? How many ELL students are there? What are their countries of origin?
2. Do I know where I can find out more about the cultural backgrounds of these students? What resources exist in my community?
3. What steps am I taking to promote my own professional development in the education of ELL students?
4. What steps have I taken to support the language and literacy development of my ELL students?
5. How do I serve as an advocate for high-quality instruction in all subject areas for the ELL students in my school?
6. What supports exist in my school to help ensure that it is a comfortable and welcoming place for ELL students?
7. What is my definition of "multiculturalism"? What do I think of when I imagine a "multicultural school"?
8. In what specific ways do I model the fair treatment of students and staff from a variety of backgrounds?

When principals understand the theory and practice of effective instruction for English-language learners, their teachers are more likely to feel supported in their use of new instructional strategies and approaches.

FACING RACE AND EQUITY ISSUES

Another serious gap in principals' professional growth programs is the lack of any explicit focus on race and equity issues. "A sad reality is that we're not doing enough. I don't think there is enough concerted, deliberate thinking about immigrant children among principals, at least not as much as there should be, given the focus on staff development under No Child Left Behind," says professional development director Jimenez. "What's lacking in the conversation is how the definition of multiculturalism or diversity has changed. For a long time it meant that you bring in the children's culture, the holidays, the ethnic traditions. That's a start, but I think the conversation has to be around why we are not bringing equity of resources to immigrant children."

As part of one of her recent professional development institutes for new principals, Jimenez provided them with cameras and instructed them to go into students' communities and take pictures of anything they thought was valued there. She also asked them to interview people in the communities about what they thought of the school. While some principals were reluctant at first, the exercise proved for many to be an eye-opening experience. Jimenez says she used the activity to highlight to the principals that they can bring "value-added perceptions" of language-minority students to their schools.

"I tell them that you need to make people conscious of the value diversity adds. If you don't, [this awareness] won't happen," Jimenez says.

Also, according to Jimenez, school principals need to be deliberate in helping teachers think about critical issues such as race and language differences, topics that are too often sidestepped in discussions about the education of language-minority children. She says that principals who are committed to the vision of academic achievement for *all* children have a clear mandate: "They must create the opportunity for the conversation, not in an accusatory manner, but they must help teachers come to terms with who they are as cultural beings."

Principal certification alone will not prepare a school leader to deal with the range of cultural, linguistic, and racial issues involved in educating language-minority children. "It's perhaps possible to come up with an 'ideal syllabus' for preparing school administrators," observes Guadalupe Guerrero. "However, you could prepare superstar graduates and they still might fall short in practice. You need to look at yourself and at your core values, and at your expectations for learning. You need to ask yourself, do you have a clear understanding of pedagogy? Are you willing to be an advocate for all students?"

The principalship is often called the loneliest job in education. A solitary search for answers to questions about ELL teaching and learning, says Gayle Jones, can be a serious barrier to effective leadership. Schools can make real progress, she says, only when the professionals working there pool their intellectual resources—and their commitment—and strive toward common goals. "You have to go with the energy you have. All administrators and teacher leaders need to understand that this is an opportunity to address the needs of *all* children and that we need to contemplate a range of possibilities," Jones says. "Together, we must remain open to change."

This chapter was supported by a grant from the Foundation for Child Development. It originally appeared in the March/April 2004 issue of the Harvard Education Letter.

REFERENCES

Elmore, R. F. (2003). *Knowing the right thing to do: School improvement and performance-based accountability.* Washington, DC: NGA Center for Best Practices.

Goldenberg, C., & Sullivan, J. (1994). *Making change happen in a language minority school: A search for coherence.* Washington, DC: National Center for Research on Cultural Diversity and Second Language Learning. Available online at www.ncela.gwu.edu/miscpubs/ncrcdsll/epr13/index.htm.

Hale, E. L., & Moorman, H. N. (2003). *Preparing school principals: A national perspective on policy and program innovations.* Washington, DC: Institute for Educational Leadership. Available online at www.iel.org/pubs.html#other.

Kindler, A. (2002). *Survey of the states' limited English proficient students and available educational programs and services, 2000–2001 summary report.* Washington, DC: National Clearinghouse for English Language Acquisition and Language Instruction Educational Programs.

FOR FURTHER INFORMATION

D. August and K. Hakuta (eds.). *Educating Language Minority Children.* Washington, DC: National Academy Press, 1998.

L.T. Diaz-Rico. *Teaching English Learners: Strategies and Methods.* Boston: Pearson, 2004.

M. Kuamoo. "Effective School Leadership . . . Like Riding a Bike." *NABE News* 26, no. 1 (September/October 2002): 6–11, 33.

CHAPTER 9

Bringing Parents on Board

Building Strong Home-School Connections with Immigrant Families

Sue Miller Wiltz

There is a Spanish saying that has slowly been gaining currency with the educators of English-language learners (ELLs): *Lo que se aprende en la cuna, siempre dura.* That which is learned in the crib lasts forever. Few programs embrace that concept more strongly than AVANCE, a nonprofit organization founded in San Antonio, Texas, in 1973 to prepare poor and primarily Latino kids for academic success by focusing on their earliest and most influential teachers—parents.*

Many researchers have noted the importance of parental involvement in the education of all students, not just immigrants. But given that immigrant parents often do not speak English and may not be familiar with the standards and cus-

*The name AVANCE is taken from the Spanish word *avance*, meaning advance.

toms of U.S. schools, getting them involved in their children's education presents special challenges for teachers and administrators. Immigrant parents may be hindered by language barriers and feelings of powerlessness. Those from cultures that put a high emphasis on obedience and respect for authority may not be comfortable approaching or questioning teachers. They also may be confused about what the schools expect of their children.

Helping immigrant parents and their preschool-age children surmount those challenges is the main mission of AVANCE's 11 chapters in Texas and California. "We stress to parents that their child's first three years are a critical time for development," says Sanjay Mathur, executive director of the organization's El Paso, Texas, chapter. He says recent immigrants often feel depressed and isolated, and are frequently overworked and underpaid. "But we talk to them about how important it is that they find time to talk to their children, listen to their problems, take them to the library, and read to them on a regular basis. Ultimately, when they realize how much they are helping their children, they become empowered."

That's what happened to Carmen Ramirez, who moved from her native Mexico to the border city of El Paso nine years ago. When she brought her older son to kindergarten at Burleson Elementary School—located in a low-income, Spanish-speaking neighborhood—an outreach coordinator pulled her aside and asked if she and her two-year-old would like to join AVANCE's Even Start family literacy program, which occupied two of the school's classrooms. "I had so much shame because I didn't speak English," says Ramirez, but she gave the program a try.

For 23 hours a week over the next nine months, Ramirez and a dozen other mothers participated in ESL, GED, and parenting classes. Just across the hall, her younger son and the other toddlers kept busy, drawing and coloring, completing puzzles, singing songs, and learning vocabulary in their native tongue as well as English. At lunch and later in the afternoon, parents and kids gathered under the supervision of AVANCE teachers, who offered them tips as they read together, made educational toys, and worked on other joint activities. "The program is truly wonderful," says Ramirez, speaking in a mix of Spanish and English. "It has helped us to learn more English, and I have become a much better mother."

Although AVANCE has parenting and other outreach programs in a church and several community centers throughout the city, Mathur says its directors like to locate the Even Start family literacy program in elementary schools so that both preschool children and their parents can adjust to the school environment before they enter kindergarten. He also believes that bringing parents into the elementary schools gets them more involved in their children's education as well as their own. The result? Last year, for example, 75 percent of AVANCE parents completed one learning level in English during the nine-month program, while 42 percent completed two or more levels. A substantial number also passed all five GED exams, and several of them are going on to college.

Their children are benefiting, too: Last year, 53 percent of the program's participants between the ages of two and four rated in the normal range of language development at the end of the year, compared with just 13 percent at the beginning. Nearly 90 percent of those transferring to another preschool or kindergarten were rated by their new teachers as "average" or "way above average" on measures of school readiness. Moreover, all first and second graders who had been in the program advanced to the next grade.

Ramirez, who earned her GED last May, now works at Burleson as an AVANCE Even Start teaching assistant helping new immigrant mothers. Her older son attends second grade down the hall, and her younger son, now four, continues in the family literacy program. She is proud of his progress in English but also works with him to build his home language.

BENEFITS OF DUAL-LANGUAGE CLASSES

In promoting English-language learning, AVANCE emphasizes a dual-language approach so that Spanish speakers develop skills in their native language and in English. "We support the bilingual philosophy," says Mathur. "But sometimes people think of literacy as only English literacy. I think that's narrow. Research has shown that children who develop a high level of literacy in their home language are subsequently more adept at transferring that literacy to English."

This approach is especially helpful in fostering home-school connections with immigrant families. Immigrant students often grow up in a split world, encountering a vastly different culture at school than they do at home. If they are foreigners in English-only classes at school, they may also begin to feel estranged at home, where their culture and language are different from what they encounter each day at school.

Dual-language instruction, such as the approach taken by AVANCE, can blunt that sense of isolation for both students and parents, says Linda Espinosa, a former elementary school principal and currently an early childhood educator at the University of Missouri, who is impressed with the organization's approach to literacy acquisition. "I think it's ideal if you get to [children] that early and work with the families to support home language and home culture," she says.

Indeed, the number of English-language learners in the United States doubled between 1990 and 2002, and they now make up nearly 10 percent of the overall school-age population, according to Patton Tabors, a researcher at the Harvard Graduate School of Education. As many as 329 different languages are spoken in the homes of these children, she says, and 77 percent are native Spanish speakers.

Tabors, author of *One Child, Two Languages*, a guide for preschool educators of ELLs, is currently conducting a longitudinal study of Spanish-speaking four-year-olds in Massachusetts, Maryland, and Puerto Rico to identify the factors related to their development of language and literacy skills. Among her baseline findings: ELLs in her U.S. group scored considerably below the norm in oral language development when compared to English monolinguals, which was to be expected. However, they also scored, on average, well below the norm in oral language development in Spanish. "These results may well point to the vulnerability of young bilingual children to language loss in the context of acquiring a societal language as their second language," says Tabors.

"THE GREAT EQUALIZER"

The need to promote literacy and language development among young bilingual children—and to shore up family involvement in education—is especially pressing in a state such as Texas, where, due to immigration, Latino "minorities" are expected to be the majority by about 2020, says James Vasquez, executive director of the Region 19 Education Service Center, the El Paso teacher and literacy support arm of the Texas Education Agency. "How do we create a 'seamless' transition to this new Texas of the 21st century? The great equalizer has been, is, and will always be education," he says.

Promoting English-language learning while preventing home-language loss is a priority for the Region 19 Head Start, where half of all the three-, four- and five-year-olds and their parents speak only Spanish. Early childhood educator Blanca Enriquez took over the program in 1986, when there were just 1,200 preschoolers at 11 sites. Today it serves 3,800 preschoolers and 213 infants and toddlers at 35 sites, and has won several state and national awards for excellence.

"[Children] must learn [English] in order to succeed, and they must learn it as soon as possible," says Enriquez. "But not at the expense of losing their home language. The home language is the one that promotes and maintains culture and the values [across] generations of family members. That is so important. It is also important that we are teaching children not to speak half English and half Spanish, but to develop each language fully."

EARLY ASSESSMENT

At Region 19 Head Start, language and literacy assessment begins the moment children walk in the preschool door. Parents fill out lengthy questionnaires about their children's home language, and every child takes the Idea Proficiency Test (IPT) in both Spanish and English to identify their language dominance and measure their baseline and language acquisition growth. (They repeat the test at the end of the year.) They are also required to take the Peabody Picture Vocabulary Test in their dominant language to assess vocabulary and the Developmental Skills Checklist to determine their math and literacy skills.

Enriquez believes that parents are critical to the Head Start program's success. They serve on local program committees. A parent board helps her and the board of directors make decisions about the budget and other critical areas of management. They volunteer in the classroom and on field trips, and many end up joining the Head Start staff. "At this age level, parents are still very protective of their children and want to be involved," Enriquez says. "And if the kids see their parents involved, they are more prone to be involved themselves."

Bringing parents on board isn't always easy—especially as children grow older. Back in the mid-1990s, former superintendent Tony Trujillo decided to turn a struggling El Paso elementary school, Hacienda Heights, into a magnet school offering a dual-language curriculum. But when he held a community meeting to discuss his idea, the parents put up stiff resistance, saying they didn't want their children learning in Spanish. "They said they could teach their children at home in Spanish," says Marvyn Luckett, who was named principal of Hacienda Heights a short time later. "They wanted them to learn only English at school."

Luckett, then a vice principal in another school district, had heard that Trujillo was looking for a principal for the troubled school. She took up the challenge in July 1996, and her first move was to ask her parent outreach coordinator to round up the parents who were most vocally opposed to the dual-language program. "Well, I got down to the old library and it was standing room only," she said. "They said, 'Why should we trust you?' I said, 'You shouldn't. Trust has to be earned. Just give me time.'"

Hacienda Heights ultimately adopted an 80/10/10 model, based on allocation of languages of instruction in the primary grades: 80 percent of instruction in Spanish, 10 percent in English, and 10 percent in a third language, either Japanese or French. While the ratio of instruction provided through the third language remains steady at 10 percent, the ratio of Spanish to English instruction gradually shifts over time until reaching a 45-45-10 ratio in the fifth grade. At first, children learn science and social studies in English and literacy and math in Spanish. Luckett explains that "literacy starts to transition to English in the third grade once they learn to read in Spanish."

Since implementing the new program, the school has experienced a complete turnaround—culminating in its selection as a National Blue Ribbon School in 2000–2001. Test scores are up among students with limited English proficiency (LEP) and non-LEP students alike; student attendance and parental involvement are high; and there is now a waiting list for kids wanting to attend Hacienda Heights.

A spacious library is now the school's architectural centerpiece, and Luckett has filled it not only with books but also with beautiful murals of children playing traditional Mexican games that are labeled in Spanish. Circulation averages 15,000 titles a month, and children have an impressive number of titles—8,000 in Spanish and more than 15,000 in English—from which to choose.

Winning parents over has been essential. "You also have to educate the parents and the community that Spanish literacy is important, that children who learn to read in their mother tongue will be more successful," says Luckett. "Reading is a non-negotiable."

Hacienda even gets its parents involved with reading the books that their kids have read, sponsoring four to six of what Luckett calls "parent book launches" each year. Nearly 100 parents show up for a night of iced tea and cookies, sitting around tables in the cafeteria as they discuss the author, illustrator, characters, and central theme while the school provides babysitting for their children in the gym. Luckett tries to choose books that are available in both English and Spanish, but "if a book isn't available in Spanish, we translate," she says. "I've seen families get very emotional, with tears in their eyes, when they respond to the literature."

OTHER OUTREACH

Other parent outreach at the school includes a School Fun Fair the Saturday before classes begin, which provides activities for the kids while the parents enjoy mini-workshops with teachers, librarians, and counselors. During the year, each student is also required to keep a log of the books she or he is reading, which parents must sign to show that they are keeping track of their child's progress. The school also hosts the Latino Family Literacy Project, which provides parents with a forum to discuss parenting concerns, education, family goals, and traditions. During the 12-session project, parents work with their children on daily reading and taking photos for a family album, using books and cameras bought by the school.

One measure of success of any program is whether its students are meeting academic achievement that is on grade level or higher. Until 2002, students at Hacienda Heights, like all students in Texas, were required to take the Texas Assessment of Academic Skills (TAAS), which was administered to students each year beginning in the third grade. Based on these scores, the Texas Education Agency issued Hacienda its highest "exemplary" rating.

However, in 2003, Texas students were required to take a new and much more rigorous test, the Texas Assessment of Knowledge and Skills (TAKS). Luckett was delighted to learn that Hacienda Heights did far better than the statewide average, with pass rates of 93 percent in writing, 89 percent in reading, and 90 percent in math. She was even more pleased that her LEP students held their own or did even better than her non-LEP students, with pass rates of 97 percent in writing, 88 percent in reading, and 86 percent in math.

To Luckett, that's just another positive sign that their dual-language formula is working. It also suggests that, with the support and involvement of parents, the prospects for Hacienda's students are brightening—which is one reason some of those parents came to Texas in the first place.

This chapter was supported by a grant from the Foundation for Child Development. It.originally appeared in the January/February 2004 issue of the Harvard Education Letter.

FOR FURTHER INFORMATION

AVANCE, Inc., 301 So. Frio Street, Suite 380, San Antonio, TX 78207; tel: 210-270-4630; fax: 210-270-4612. www.avance.org

L.M. Espinosa. "Hispanic Parent Involvement in Early Childhood Programs." ERIC Clearinghouse on Elementary and Early Childhood Education. Urbana: University of Illinois at Urbana-Champaign, 1995. Available online at http://ericeece.org.

L.M. Espinosa and M.S. Burns. "Early Literacy for Young Children and English Language Learners," in *Teaching 4- to 8-Year-Olds: Literacy, Math, Multiculturalism and Classroom Community,* ed. C. Howes. Baltimore: Paul H. Brookes, 2003.

M. Suárez-Orozco and C. Suárez-Orozco. *Children of Immigration.* Cambridge, MA: Harvard University Press, 2001.

P.O. Tabors. *One Child, Two Languages: A Guide for Preschool Educators of Children Learning English as a Second Language.* Baltimore: Brookes, 1997.

P.O. Tabors, M.M. Paez, and L.M. Lopez. "Dual Language Abilities of Bilingual Four-Year-Olds: Initial Findings from the Early Childhood Study of Language and Literacy Development of Spanish-Speaking Children." *NABE Journal of Research and Practice* (Winter 2003).

CHAPTER 10

On Nobody's Agenda

Improving English-Language Learners' Access to Higher Education

Rebecca M. Callahan and Patricia Gándara

Most young people in the United States go on to college or some kind of postsecondary training after completing high school (American Council on Education, 2003; Wirt et al., 2003). It is increasingly difficult in this information- and technology-based economy to gain an economic foothold without some postsecondary preparation. However, if a student has not mastered English, he or she is likely to be channeled into dead-end classes that emphasize English-language acquisition to the exclusion of courses that prepare students for high school graduation or postsecondary opportunities (Callahan, 2003; Ruiz-de-Velasco & Fix, 2000). Such a truncated education places these English-language learners (ELLs) at a social and economic disadvantage for the rest of their lives, and it creates impediments to social mobility for their children (Grogger & Trejo, 2002). The consequences for society as a whole are also far reaching. To the extent that ELLs are not adequately educated to contribute meaningfully to the economy, social service burdens increase and tax revenues decrease (Hayes-Bautista, Schink, & Chapa, 1988). To break this cycle of under-education requires focused attention on the specific academic needs of these students, yet we find that the education of secondary-level ELLs is really on nobody's agenda.

U.S. Census data from 2000 indicate that the number of ELLs in U.S. schools has increased by 46 percent in the past decade, while the number of 5- to 17-year-olds has increased by only 17 percent in the same time period.[1] Researchers have noted that the majority of growth in the school-age population over the past two decades can be attributed to immigration—both immigrant children and children of immigrants (Camarota, 2001). Today, almost three-fourths of all teachers nationwide have at least one ELL in their classroom (Zehler et al., 2003). The education of ELLs has become everybody's issue, and yet painfully little has been done to address these students' needs.

National data on ELLs are notoriously unreliable, in part because definitions and measures of language proficiency vary so widely across the states (Council of Chief State School Officers, 1992), and in part because there is great variation in data collection by region. However, statistics from California—the state with the largest number and percentage of ELLs in the country—can provide some important insights into this population. In California, about 18 percent of ELLs are found in secondary schools, and despite their very high rates of attrition from high school, secondary ELL students are the fastest-growing sector of the ELL population. This is attributable to at least two causes in addition to actual influxes of immigrant students: 1) retention within the ELL program because of inability to meet academic exit requirements, and 2) retention at grade level and failure to graduate (Freeman, Freeman, & Mercuri, 2002; Secada et al., 1998; Waggoner, 1999).

According to the 2003 California English Language Development Test (CELDT), roughly two-thirds (65.8%) of seventh- to twelfth-grade ELLs report having been enrolled in U.S. schools for seven years or more, and more than half (54.4%) of these students score at an advanced or early advanced level on the CELDT. Thus, for most, acquisition of basic English is not the primary factor in their long-term ELL status. Rather, the greater obstacles these students face relate to subject-matter knowledge and the acquisition of academic English—the more sophisticated form of the language that gives students the tools to analyze, think, and write critically (Scarcella & Rumberger, 2000; Snow, 2004; Wong-Fillmore & Snow, 2000).

A PROBLEM OF ACCESS

So while access to higher education for ELLs is a significant problem, perhaps an even more pressing problem for these students is their lack of access to *any* kind of meaningful education in secondary school. A variety of structural barriers in place within schools block ELLs' access to a curriculum that will ensure a high school diploma and realistic postsecondary options. Among the school factors that limit the academic growth of linguistic-minority students are inadequate teacher preparation (Walqui, 2000), lack of access and exposure to rigorous academic curriculum (Lucas, Henze, & Donato, 1990), limited and erratic ELL support services (Fleischman & Hopstock, 1993; Minicucci & Olsen, 1992; Zehler et al., 2003), and insufficient time to accomplish the tasks of high school (Gándara, 2000; Snow, 2004).

Underlying all of these school-related factors is an even more fundamental problem—the lack of any articulated goals for these students or a plan to prepare them for higher education. Without clear goals, any improvement in the education of ELLs is bound to be elusive. Yet, it is common for school districts and states to have no particular program goals other than to "close the achievement gap." If policymakers simply want to ensure that ELLs become orally proficient in English within a specified amount of time, oral fluency in English is the first step on the ladder to language proficiency and may be acquired in three to five years (Hakuta, Butler, & Witt, 2000; Thomas & Collier, 2002), regardless of the type of program students are in. Both bilingual and English-only programs appear to achieve this in similar amounts of time (Willig, 1985). However, English oral fluency does not ensure that students can do grade-level academic work. To master academic content in English, students need to gain *academic* English proficiency. Under normal circumstances this generally takes from four to seven years, according to researchers (Hakuta et al., 2000; Thomas & Collier, 2002).

Schools' unwritten and generally unarticulated goals for ELLs are essentially twofold: for recent immigrants, the goal is to teach them English; for long-term ELLs, the goal is dropout prevention and—in the best-case scenario—high school graduation. If and when ELLs do graduate from high school prepared to enter higher education, it is almost always as a result of a program initiated by an individual or a group expressly interested in the academic achievement of ELLs, rather than a systematic change in the larger school structure

(Spaulding, Carolino, & Amen, 2004). With a few notable exceptions, the task of preparing ELLs for college has never found its way onto the agenda of any key players in the secondary school system, or, for that matter, in higher education. Because most programs for secondary ELLs are not driven by explicit academic goals, curriculum is often haphazard and dependent upon whatever local resources are readily available. Being in dead-end courses with weak curricula, isolated from the rest of the students on the campus, it is no wonder why so many high-school-age ELLs simply drop out (Mehan, 1997; Ruiz-de-Velasco & Fix, 2000; Secada et al., 1998).

BARRIERS TO POSTSECONDARY EDUCATION

Even for the ELL students who persist in high school, the deck is stacked against their ever being able to attain a college degree. Based on our research, we believe that English-language learners' lack of preparation for higher education results not so much from their limited English skills as from inherent barriers in the structure and content of their schooling.

Inadequately Trained Teachers

First, an inordinately high proportion of teachers who teach ELLs have no specialized training to meet these students' needs. According to research led by Annette Zehler, a researcher at Development Associates, more than 70 percent of teachers who teach three or more ELLs have no ELL-specific teaching credential. Zehler and her colleagues also found that 61 percent of teachers teaching three or more ELLs had received some professional development geared toward the needs of ELLs, but the median amount of such training was just four hours over a five-year period (Zehler et al., 2003, p. 13). Less than an hour of training per year will not and cannot fully prepare teachers to meet the academic and linguistic needs of these students. The situation in California, where we have collected extensive data on teacher preparation, is even greater reason for concern. In the state with the nation's largest concentration of ELLs, these students are more than twice as likely as other poor students, and many times more likely than affluent students, to be taught by a teacher who is completely uncertified to teach *any* student (Gándara, Rumberger, Maxwell-Jolly, & Callahan, 2003).

Limited Access to Academic Content

Whether or not teachers are trained either with a basic teaching credential or with ELL-specific training, schools must also have an infrastructure in place to support the academic development of ELLs and their acquisition of English. In an earlier review of services for limited English proficient (LEP) students, Howard Fleischman, also of Development Associates, found a predominance of pullout English as a Second Language (ESL) programs, which suggests that when ELLs did receive services, it was in lieu of their normal academic instruction rather than integrated into the regular academic day. The exchange of classroom instruction for ESL pullout services results in these students receiving less direct academic instruction than their native English-speaking counterparts. It has been argued that ELLs in particular, and poor and minority students in general, simply need more focused instructional time in order to both develop linguistic strengths and bring their skills up to par academically with native English speakers (Gándara, 2000). ESL pullout programs are just as prevalent today (Zehler et al., 2003) as they were a decade ago (Fleischman & Hopstock, 1993)—if not more so—which demonstrates that ELLs' exposure to academic content continues to be limited by inefficient ways of organizing their instruction.

Beyond ESL pullout at the elementary level, academic isolation continues through secondary school. Sample EL transcripts, like that shown in Figure 1, illustrate the primarily non-academic nature of students' schedules, with work study and low-level content area courses dominating their program.

Weak Language Instruction

In addition to limited academic preparation, ELLs also experience limited instruction in academic literacy. Traditional ESL or English-language development (ELD) programs focus on the development of basic English proficiency, rarely progressing to instruction in academic literacy skills. At the secondary level, language acquisition programs often prove to be at odds with the academic needs of long-term ELLs, while they simultaneously lack the specific literacy skill instruction recent immigrants need to be able to read and write across the content areas (Freeman et al., 2002). Long-term ELLs' permanency in ELL programs is often a result of an inability to demonstrate grade-level academic competence (Linquanti, 2001), and placement in traditional ESL/ELD curriculum, as it is routinely organized, will not help them achieve those levels of academic competence.

Weak Curriculum

When students are labeled as ELLs or LEP, this typically signals the schools to decrease the difficulty level of their course work in order to compensate for the students' perceived lin-

FIGURE 1
SAMPLE HIGH SCHOOL SCHEDULES FOR FOUR ENGLISH-LANGUAGE LEARNERS FROM TWO DISTRICTS

DISTRICT #1

Saul

- Sophomore
- 2 years in the U.S.
- Attended 9th grade in Mexico, where he took college preparatory curriculum and advanced mathematics courses

Period 1: No class
Period 2: Language Development 1
Period 3: Language Development 2
Period 4: Native Spanish 1
Period 5: U.S. History (in Spanish)
Period 6: Math A (general, low level)
Period 7: Weightlifting

Two courses, Spanish and U.S. History, meet college preparatory requirements; no science.

Jose Luis

- Sophomore
- 1 year in the U.S.
- Uneven academic history prior to immigration

Period 1: No class
Period 2: Language Development 1
Period 3: Language Development 2
Period 4: General Math (in English)
Period 5: Native Spanish 1
Period 6: Drawing 1
Period 7: No class

One class, Spanish, prepares student for college requirements; no science or social studies. Student failed English-only math because he could not understand the teacher.

FIGURE 1, CONTINUED

DISTRICT #2

Marcos

- Sophomore
- Long-term English learner
- Enrolled in California schools prior to entering high school

Period 1: English 10 SDAIE*
Period 2: World History SDAIE
Period 3: Pre-Algebra A SDAIE
Period 4: Court Sports
Period 5: Integrated Science 2 SDAIE
Period 6: ELD** 5

Only two courses could be used to meet college preparatory requirements, World History and Integrated Science (as an elective, not as a science course). Student never took a college preparatory science, math, or English course through the junior year of high school.

Marisela

- Senior
- Long-term English learner
- Enrolled in California schools prior to entering high school

Period 1: Power English
Period 2: Weight Training
Period 3: ELD 5C
Period 4: Business Math
Period 5: Consumer Foods
Period 6: Floral Design

None of the student's courses meets college preparatory criteria. The student took no laboratory science or math beyond Algebra 1, which she failed and for which she received no credit.

* Specially Designed Academic Instruction in English
** English-Language Development

guistic "deficiency." ELLs are generally placed in the ESL track with ELL-specific course work, such as specially designed academic instruction in English and sheltered instruction, that often is neither academically rigorous nor adequate for college entry (Minicucci & Olsen, 1993). If these students manage to graduate from high school, and many do not (Ruiz-de-Velasco & Fix, 2000), their high school transcripts often document a secondary career that leaves them ill prepared to enter higher education.

Figure 1 shows four randomly selected student schedules typical of both long-term ELLs and recent immigrants. At most, one or two of the classes an English learner takes in a semester will meet the criteria for being designated "college preparatory," far below the two-thirds ratio needed in California to meet university entry requirements. In addition, the college preparatory courses in which ELLs are likely to find themselves are assigned more for reasons of convenience in scheduling than as part of a coherent college-preparation plan.

A recent study in one Northern California high school with more than 350 ELLs revealed that, on average, these students did not complete even half of the minimum college preparatory requirements (Callahan, 2003, p. 71). Fewer than 4 percent had enrolled in the minimal course work requirements necessary to apply to a four-year university. In addition, only one senior in the graduating cohort of 68 went on to enroll in a four-year university.

Math and science preparation is especially important for students hoping to enter higher education (Center for Higher Education Policy Analysis, 1998; Gándara & Bial, 2001). These content areas are usually less language dependent and are therefore among the only accessible non-ESL classes in which ELLs can enroll. Yet in the Northern California study cited earlier, only 16 percent of the tenth- to twelfth-grade ELLs sampled had taken either geometry or Integrated Laboratory Science II, key gatekeeper courses to college preparatory course work, and just 10 percent had taken both of these courses (Callahan, 2003). In a descriptive study of a variety of college preparatory programs in a central California high school, Anysia Mayer of the University of California at Davis (2003) found that ELLs are denied access to all but one of the district's college preparatory programs. The one program open to ELLs enrolls, at best, 10 percent of the district's secondary ELLs in a given grade.

LINGUISTIC ISOLATION

ELLs are highly segregated from English speakers, and they are grouped in classrooms in which their fellow students are also limited in English (Ruiz-de-Velasco & Fix, 2000) and where there are few opportunities to interact with native English-speaking models. Without such contact, an important source of language modeling is lost. Additionally, "social capital"—knowledge of the schooling system and familiarity with the people in authority in it—that is routinely shared among English speakers is absent in these environments, putting these students at greater educational risk. Relegated to low-track classrooms, ELLs' linguistic isolation does not begin at the secondary level. Data from the federal government's Early Childhood Longitudinal Study (ECLS:K)[2] shows that more than half (57.2%) of kindergarten ELLs in a 1998 national sample attended school in classrooms consisting of over 50 percent limited English–speaking peers. Also, in a study of

ELLs in a rural California high school ESL classroom, researcher Clayton Hurd (2004) illustrated how the marginalization of these students resulted in antischooling behaviors. In a setting in which peer acceptance was based more on challenging adult authority figures (whom they perceived as often denigrating their self-worth) than on engaging in classroom learning, students behaved in ways that undermined any possibility of school success.

Linguistic and academic isolation also results in a type of peer-group isolation that often places ELLs outside of the college-going discourse and limits their exposure to information about postsecondary options. A 2004 study by Gándara, Gutierrez, and O'Hara showed how the career and schooling aspirations of low-income, rural Latino students were narrowly constructed to include only the very limited options they had observed in their own communities. Most of these students never talked about school or future options among themselves, while this was a major topic of conversation and source of information among their middle-class white peers.

Insufficient Time

Another major obstacle to ELLs' college access is time. The current structure of schooling, at both the elementary and secondary levels, lacks the flexibility to permit these students to develop both linguistic and academic proficiency in the time allotted (Gándara, 2000). Recent immigrants have been shown to succeed at the high school level when given additional time to master geometry and biology in addition to English (Ruiz-de-Velasco & Fix, 2000). Schools currently expect that ELLs will both learn English and master academic content within the same timeframe and under the same constraints as their English-only peers, and label them as below grade level and at risk when they do not.

To be sure, providing the additional time that ELLs need to succeed in learning both English and academic content will involve nothing less than a social and academic transformation in U.S. schools. As Harvard professor Catherine Snow, whose research focuses on language and literacy development, has noted:

> Providing additional time, and ensuring that each child receives expert instruction, is expensive. But students cannot learn what they are not taught. Transforming English language learners into good readers and academic achievers requires increased resources and commitment, both from those who run the schools and from the citizens and communities that pay for them. (2004, p. 4)

Without serious restructuring, schools will not advance toward the practices necessary to allow ELLs to master both critical skill areas.

BREAKING THE MOLD: EXEMPLARY PROGRAMS

While the overall picture we paint is bleak, we do know that some ELLs manage not only to graduate from high school, but also to enroll in four-year universities and even go on to have successful academic careers. Here we profile several programs that successfully move ELLs through the high school curriculum and into college. It is important to note, however, that these programs exist and are successful because an individual or a group of individuals at a school recognized the problem and took systematic steps to alter the existing school structure. Beyond having dedicated individuals at the school-site level, these programs all incorporate what we believe are fundamental requirements if ELLs are to be academically successful: modified instructional strategies, exposure to rigorous academic curriculum, extracurricular integration, extra time (perhaps the most important element), and—in many cases—schoolwide reform.

New York City: Perhaps the most highly lauded secondary school reform to benefit ELLs is that of the International High School (IHS) programs in New York. Shelley Spaulding and her colleagues at the Council of Chief State School Officers in Washington, D.C., report that the IHS "partnership schools have success rates of over 90 percent in high school graduation, course passage and college acceptance" (Spaulding, Carolino, & Amen, 2004, p. 34). Recent immigrant ELLs enrolled in these programs take a rigorous college preparatory course load with teachers who modify instruction to meet their specific linguistic needs (Nadelstern, 1986; Walqui, 2000). Teachers draw on and encourage students to develop primary language skills, with biliteracy as a primary goal. In the IHS programs, the first two years are spent in a Junior Institute, in which language skills are developed. Upon demonstrating task mastery in the four main content areas, students then move into the Senior Institute, where they focus on the content standards of the New York State Regents exam (Spaulding et al., 2004). Teachers are given the opportunity to develop curricula that meet the linguistic needs of the students as well as the content area standards. A key focus beyond academics and language is the development of students' "habits of mind," an integration of academic skills into everyday life (Spaulding et al., 2004). The attention paid to the development of the student as a whole—academically, linguistically, and as a learner—may be key to the success of the IHS programs with recent immigrant ELLs.

Stockton, California: While IHS programs were developed as a method of whole-school reform, other efforts have been made to develop a program specifically for ELLs within a larger school context. Franklin High School, located in the poorest barrio of Stockton, California, offers an Academia de Español for recent immigrants who demonstrate strong academic promise (Bello, Alonzo, & Alonzo, 1997). The students follow a structured college-preparatory program, receiving primary language instruction in core content academics for the first two years of high school and in English during the last two years. After four years of program implementation, none of the ELLs participating in the Academia program held below a C average, and most earned at least a B average. Students are expected to spend extra time performing both community service and academic tutoring. At the time of the four-year evaluation of Academia (Bello et al., 1997), nine of the 25 graduating seniors had already been accepted to a four-year university, and all planned to go to college.

Florida: Project GOTCHA (Galaxies of Thinking and Creative Heights of Achievement), started in Florida for students up to eighth grade, identifies and serves gifted ELLs. The program incorporates creative thinking and problem-solving with Howard Gardner's multiple intelligences theory. It serves identified students, generally clustered by language proficiency, for at least two hours per week in a separate classroom and is sometimes incorporated into students' mainstream classes (Aguirre & Hernández, 2002). While operating only into middle school, this type of program sets the stage for ELLs to move seamlessly into college preparatory curricula in high school. Our own research has shown that the likelihood of minority students being placed in college preparatory curricula in secondary school is greatly enhanced by participation in gifted and talented programs before high school (Gándara, in press).

CLEARING THE PATH: ARTICULATING AN ACADEMIC AGENDA

Virtually all programs that succeed in improving the post-secondary prospects of ELLs depend on a group of dedicated school personnel who take it upon themselves to either change the infrastructure of the school itself, alter the mind-set of the teachers and staff, or both. When systematic, structural change cannot occur schoolwide, smaller, more individual-dependent programs such as Academia serve to modify a small segment of the school agenda to meet the needs of a few ELLs. Key to the success of ELLs in all these programs is an explicit plan articulating their exposure to high-level academic content and curriculum. ELLs' preparation for higher education becomes a part of everyone's agenda in these cases. In addition, time is a key element, as ELLs are offered supplemental instruction during evenings, weekends, and summers to further their academic growth and spend extra time in structured academic, linguistic, and extracurricular contexts (Spaulding et al., 2004).

All of the programs mentioned here incorporate what we believe are the three most important strategies for involving high school ELLs in the culture and discourse of higher education: placement in rigorous academic curriculum, use of the primary language as a resource, and extended instructional time. Other schools and districts are beginning to recognize the fundamental structural barriers that prevent ELLs' access to rigorous academic preparation. While programmatic changes may not happen overnight, there is some evidence of progress. Some schools, for example, have begun to require before- or afterschool instruction for ELLs enrolled in ESL (T. Morales, personal communication, April 25, 2004); others do not allow ELLs to work as teacher or office assistants in lieu of academic course work. Despite small changes at the local level and the handful of exemplary programs described here, the lack of articulation between high school ELL programs and college preparatory requirements leaves the majority of ELLs "on the outside looking in" with regard to higher education.

If policymakers are serious about ELLs reaching the same level of overall academic proficiency as native English speakers—that is, really closing the achievement gap—this almost certainly requires additional resources. English-language learners cannot be expected to master both English and an English-based academic curriculum in the same amount of time and with the same resources as English-speaking students. The programs provided for ELLs should be driven by clear and explicit goals for their academic and linguistic outcomes and a real commitment to placing college access for English-language learners on our national agenda.

REFERENCES

American Council on Education. (2003). *Minorities in higher education 2002–2003: Twentieth annual status report*. Washington, DC: Author.

Aguirre, N., & Hernández, N. (2002). Portraits of success: Programs that work. In J. Castellano & E. Diaz (Eds.), *Reaching new horizons: Gifted and talented education for culturally and linguistically diverse students* (pp. 200–219). Boston: Allyn & Bacon.

Bello, S., Alonzo, J., & Alonzo, A. (1997). *Academia de Español case study: An Hispanic success story*. Stockton, CA: Franklin High School.

Callahan, R. M. (2003). *Opportunity to learn in a California high school: Track placement and English learners*. Davis: University of California at Davis.

Camarota, S. (2001). *The impact of immigration on U.S. population growth*. Paper presented at the U.S. House of Representatives Committee on the Judiciary Subcommittee on Immigration, Border Security, and Claims, Washington, DC.

Council of Chief State School Officers. (1992). *Recommendations for improving the assessment and monitoring of students with limited English proficiency*. Washington, DC: Author.

Center for Higher Education Policy Analysis. (1998). *National study of college preparation programs: Program summary*. Los Angeles: Author.

Fleischman, H. L., & Hopstock, P. J. (1993). *Descriptive study of services to limited English proficient students*. Arlington, VA: Development Associates.

Freeman, Y. S., Freeman, D. E., & Mercuri, S. (2002). *Closing the achievement gap: How to reach limited-formal-schooling and long-term English learners*. Portsmouth, NH: Heinemann.

Gándara, P. C. (2000). *The dimensions of time and the challenge of school reform*. Albany: State University of New York Press.

Gándara, P. C. (in press). *Creating models of high achievement for Latino students*. Storrs, CT: National Research Center on the Gifted and Talented.

Gándara, P. C., & Bial, D. (2001). *Paving the way to postsecondary education: K–12 intervention programs for underrepresented youth* (Report No. NCES2001205). Washington, DC: National Center for Education Statistics.

Gándara, P. C., Gutierrez, D., & O'Hara, S. (2004). The changing shape of aspirations: Mexican American students and the influence of peers on future plans. In M. A. Gibson, P. Gándara, & J. P. Koyama (Eds.), *School connections: U.S. Mexican youth, peers, and school achievement*. New York: Teachers College Press.

Gándara, P. C., Rumberger, R. W., Maxwell-Jolly, J., & Callahan, R. M. (2003). English learners in California schools: Unequal resources, unequal outcomes. *Education Policy Analysis Archives, 11*(36).

Grogger, J., & Trejo, S. J. (2002). *Falling behind or moving up? The intergenerational progress of Mexican Americans*. San Francisco: Public Policy Institute of California.

Hakuta, K., Butler, Y. G., & Witt, D. (2000). *How long does it take English learners to attain proficiency?* Santa Barbara: University of California Linguistic Minority Research Institute.

Hayes-Bautista, D., Schink, W., & Chapa, J. (1988). *The burden of support: Young Latinos in an aging society.* Palo Alto, CA: Stanford University Press.

Hurd, C. (2004). "Acting out" and being a "schoolboy": Performance in an ELD classroom. In M. A. Gibson, P. Gándara, & J. P. Koyama (Eds.), *School connections: U.S. Mexican youth, peers and school achievement*. New York: Teachers College Press.

Kindler, A. (2002). *Survey of the states' limited English proficient students and available educational programs and services: 2000–2001 summary report*. Washington, DC: National Clearinghouse for English Language Acquisition and Language Instruction Educational Programs.

Linquanti, R. (2001). *The redesignation dilemma: Challenges and choices in fostering meaningful accountability for English learners* (Policy Report No. 2001-1). San Francisco: WestEd, University of California Linguistic Minority Research Institute.

Lucas, T., Henze, R., & Donato, R. (1990). Promoting the success of Latino language minority students: An exploratory study of six high schools. *Harvard Educational Review, 60*, 315–340.

Mayer, A. P. (2003). *A descriptive study of five college prep programs in an urban high school: Applying action theory.* Unpublished master's thesis, University of California at Davis, Davis, CA.

Mehan, H. (1997). *Contextual factors surrounding Hispanic dropouts, 1997.* Available online at www.ncbe.gwu.edu/miscpubs/hdp/1/index.htm.

Minicucci, C., & Olsen, L. (1992). *Programs for secondary limited English proficient students: A California study*. Washington, DC: National Clearinghouse for Bilingual Education.

Minicucci, C., & Olsen, L. (1993). Caught unawares: California secondary schools confront the immigrant student challenge. *Multicultural Education, 1*(2), 16–19.

Nadelstern, E. (1986). *The International High School at LaGuardia Community College: Bridging the gap*. New York: Author. (ERIC Document 270983)

Ruiz-de-Velasco, J., & Fix, M. (2000). *Overlooked and underserved: Immigrant students in U.S. secondary schools*. Washington, DC: Urban Institute.

Scarcella, R., & Rumberger, R. W. (2000). Academic English key to long term success in school. *UC Linguistic Minority Research Institute Newsletter, 9*, 1–2.

Secada, W. G., Chavez-Chavez, R., García, E. E., Muñoz, C., Oakes, J., Santiago-Santiago, I., & Slavin, R. (1998). *No more excuses: The final report of the Hispanic Dropout Project*. Washington, DC: U.S. Department of Education, Hispanic Dropout Project.

Slavin, R., & Cheung, A. (2003). *Synthesis for research on beginning reading programs for English language learners* (Grant No. OERI-R-117-40005). Washington, DC: U.S. Department of Education, Institution of Education Sciences.

Snow, C. E. (2004). English language learners: Boosting academic achievement. *Research Points, 2*(1), 1–4.

Spaulding, S., Carolino, B., & Amen, K. (2004). *Immigrant students and secondary school reform: Compendium of best practices*. Washington, DC: Council of Chief State School Officers.

Thomas, W. P., & Collier, V. P. (2002). *A national study of school effectiveness for language minority students' long-term academic achievement: Final report. Project 1.1*. Santa Cruz, CA: Center for Research on Education, Diversity & Excellence.

Waggoner, D. (1999). Who are secondary newcomer and linguistically different youth? In C. J. Faltis & P. Wolfe (Eds.), *So much to say: Ado-*

lescents, bilingualism and ESL in the secondary school (pp. 13–41). New York: Teachers College Press.

Walqui, A. (2000). *Access and engagement: Program design and instructional approaches for immigrant students in secondary school*. McHenry, IL: Center for Applied Linguistics and Delta Systems.

Willig, A. C. (1985). A meta-analysis of selected studies on the effectiveness of bilingual education. *Review of Educational Research, 55,* 269–318.

Wirt, J., Choy, S., Provasnik, S., Rooney, P., Sen, A., & Tobin, R. (2003). *Condition of education 2003* (Report No. 2003067). Washington, DC: National Center for Educational Statistics.

Wong-Fillmore, L., & Snow, C. E. (2000). *What teachers need to know about language* (Report No. ED444379). Washington, DC: Center for Applied Linguistics, Office of Educational Research and Improvement.

Zehler, A., Fleischman, H. L., Hopstock, P. J., Stephenson, T. G., Pendzick, M. L., & Sapru, S. (2003). *Descriptive study of services to LEP students and LEP students with disabilities*. Arlington, VA: Development Associates.

NOTES

1. 2000 Census: Summary File 3, Table P19. Age by Language Spoken at Home by Ability to Speak English for the Population 5 Years and Over [67]; 1990 Census: Summary Tape File 3, Table P028. Age by Language Spoken at Home and Ability to Speak English.
2. ECLS:K Early Childhood Longitudinal Study: Kindergarten base year, National Center of Education Statistics (NCES): http://nces.ed.gov/ecls/.

About the Contributors

Rebecca M. Callahan completed her Ph.D. in education with an emphasis on second-language acquisition at the University of California, Davis, in 2003. She received a post-doctoral research fellowship from the American Educational Research Association and the U.S. Department of Education's Institute of Education Sciences. She spent the first year of the fellowship working at the University of California, Santa Barbara, in the Linguistic Minority Research Institute. She is currently continuing her fellowship at the University of Texas, Austin, in the Population Research Center. Her research includes analysis of statewide proficiency data, work with the Early Childhood Longitudinal Study database, and high school English-language learner course-taking patterns.

Donald Freeman is dean of graduate and professional studies in language teacher education at the School for International Training in Brattleboro, Vermont, where he also directs the Center for Teacher Education, Training, and Research. He writes widely on teacher learning, professional development, and teacher research. He serves on the editorial boards of the *Modern Language Journal* and *Educational Researcher*. A past president of Teachers of English to Speakers of Other Languages, Inc. (TESOL), he is a board member of the TESOL International Research Foundation as well as the International Advisory Council for the University of Cambridge ESOL Examinations (UK). He has published in various journals and in collections on teacher education. He is the editor of the *TeacherSource* series for Heinle/Thomson and is the author of *Doing Teacher Research: From Inquiry to Understanding* (Heinle/Thomson, 1998). He is also the editor of *Teacher Learning in Language Teaching* (with J. C. Richards, Cambridge University Press, 1996). His current work focuses on the relationships among teacher learning, school change, and student learning.

Patricia Gándara has been a professor of education at the University of California, Davis, for the past 15 years. She is also director of the Institute on Education Policy, Law, and Government at UC Davis, associate director of the UC Linguistic Minority Research Institute, and co-director of PACE (Policy Analysis for California Education), a Stanford University/ University of California consortium for policy research. Her primary areas of scholarship are equitable access to education (K–postsecondary) and language policy. In addition, she has been a social scientist with the RAND Corporation, director of education research in the California Legislative Assembly, and commissioner for postsecondary education for the state of California. Recent publications include *School Connections: U.S. Mexican Youth, Peers, and Achievement* (with M. Gibson & J. Koyama, Teachers College Press, 2004), "Learning English in California: Guideposts for the Nation" in *Latinos: Remaking America* (edited by M. Suárez-Orozco & M. Paez, University of California Press, 2002), and *Latino Achievement: Identifying Models That Foster Success* (National Center for Gifted and Talented Education, forthcoming).

Meg Gebhard is an assistant professor at the University of Massachusetts Amherst and codirector the ACCELA (Access to Critical Content and English Language Acquisition) master's degree program. Her interests include second-language literacies, the professional development of teachers of multilingual students, and the impact of school reforms on the education of diverse learners and the work of their teachers. She has published articles in the *TESOL Quarterly, Modern Language Journal,* and *Education Leaders*.

Andrew Habana Hafner has worked in education for the past 12 years as a classroom teacher, trainer, curriculum developer, and school administrator in domestic and international contexts. His instructional experiences and interests revolve primarily around language teaching and learning, and their intersections with larger issues of social justice and school reform. He has experience as a school principal and administrative consultant working on schoolwide management and policy reforms in conjunction with teacher and curriculum development. He is currently pursuing a doctorate in Language, Literacy and Culture at the University of Massachusetts Amherst and works in support of teacher-researchers studying language theory, qualitative research methods, and instructional methodology for supporting English-language learners.

Mary T. Jeannot is an associate professor and director of the master's degree program in teaching English as a Second Language at Gonzaga University in Spokane, Washington. Her major area of interest is the growing interdisciplinary nature of the TESOL profession and the impact that poststructuralism and critical theory have had on research and practice in the field. More immediately, her research investigates how teacher-training programs respond to the diversity represented among English speakers and teachers around the world.

Reino Makkonen is a former assistant editor of the *Harvard Education Letter* and is now an education writer and editor based in the San Francisco Bay Area. Prior to earning a master's degree at the Harvard Graduate School of Education in 2004, he spent several years working as a journalist, textbook editor, and substitute teacher in North Carolina and Massachusetts.

Michael Sadowski is the editor of the *Harvard Education Letter* and of the recent book, *Adolescents at School: Perspectives on Youth, Identity, and Education* (Harvard Education Press, 2003). He is the recipient of the Association of Educational Publishers' 2004 award for Best Learned Article and the 2002 National Press Club Award for Outstanding Newsletter Journalism, both for his work in the *Harvard Education Letter*. Michael is also an instructor and advanced doctoral candidate at the Harvard Graduate School of Education and a former high school teacher.

Maricel G. Santos is a research associate with the National Center for the Study of Adult Learning and Literacy (NCSALL) in Cambridge, Massachusetts. Her research and teaching interests include second-language vocabulary development, academic language proficiency, and the instructional needs of second-year English-language learners making the transition from language-based instruction to academic content instruction.

Evangeline Harris Stefanakis is a faculty member in learning and teaching and associate professor of research at Teachers College, Columbia University. As an international researcher and program developer who specializes in applying theory to practice, she has helped lead major school reform projects for organizations such as Project Zero (at the Harvard Graduate School of Education), the Massachusetts Department of Education, and Athens College in Athens and Salonika, Greece. She works with multicultural school communities to redesign curriculum and assessment for students with bilingual and special educational needs. Her current curriculum and assessment research projects are based in Cambridge, Mass., New York, and Athens. As a researcher, teacher educator, and writer, her work focuses on understanding how best to assess and teach children from diverse language, learning, and cultural backgrounds. She was a faculty member at the Harvard Graduate School of Education for 11 years.

Shaun Sutner is an education and political journalist based in central Massachusetts. He has been a staff reporter for the *Worcester* (Mass.) *Telegram & Gazette* since 1992 and has covered education policy, special education reform, charter schools, and school funding issues. Before joining the *Telegram & Gazette*, he worked as a staff writer for the *Washington Post*, for which he covered the District of Columbia school board.

Greta Vollmer is an assistant professor of English and applied linguistics at Sonoma State University in Rohnert Park, California. Her research has focused on such areas as second-language acquisition and pedagogy, discourse studies, and composition theory and pedagogy. She also is active in the National Writing Project as a teacher-consultant and serves on the editorial board of *TESL-EJ* (*Teaching English as a Second Language Electronic Journal*). Her recent publications include "Writing and Reflection: A Promising Start" in *The Wisdom of Practice* (edited by T. Fox, University of California Press, 2004), "Sociocultural Perspectives on Second-Language Writing" in the *ERIC/CLL News Bulletin*, "Praise and Stigma: Teachers' Constructions of the 'ESL Student'" in the *Journal of Intercultural Studies*, and "Revising Words, Revising Worlds" in *The Quarterly of the National Writing Project*. She has taught at the graduate, undergraduate and secondary levels and has worked as a teacher trainer in China, Turkey, and Italy.

Sue Miller Wiltz is a journalist who spent more than a decade as New York correspondent for *Newsweek* and *People Weekly*, reporting for hundreds of feature articles. Now based in Indianapolis, she covered the capital murder trial of John Edward Robinson Sr. for CourtTV.com and wrote a true-crime biography about Robinson. She currently edits a group of monthly newsletters for Angie's List, focusing on topics of interest to homeowners.

Mary Wright has been an elementary teacher in the Holyoke, Mass., public schools since 1992 and has taught ESL for the past ten years. In addition to her work as a teacher, Mary is currently a master's degree candidate in the ACCELA (Access to Critical Content and English Language Acquisition) program at the University of Massachusetts Amherst.